W9-BEA-964

9 5 8 1 3

0.1992

EVERYDAY FAITH

KARL RAHNER

EVERYDAY FAITH

HERDER AND HERDER

SCHOLASTICATE
ST. MARY'S UNIVERSITY
SAN ANTONIO   TEXAS

1968
Herder and Herder New York
232 Madison Avenue,
New York, N. Y. 10016

Burns & Oates Ltd.
25 Ashley Place
London S. W. 1

Palm Publishers
1949 — 55th Avenue,
Dorval — Montreal, P. Q.

Original edition:
"Glaube, der die Erde liebt", Herder Freiburg 1966

Translated by:
W. J. O'Hara

Nihil obstat: John M. T. Barton, S. T. D., L. S. S., Censor

Imprimatur: † Patrick J. Casey, Vic. Gen.
Westminster, 22nd August 1967

The Nihil obstat and Imprimatur are a declaration that a book
or pamphlet is considered to be free from doctrinal
or moral error.
It is not implied that those who have granted the Nihil obstat
and Imprimatur agree with the contents, opinions
or statements expressed.

Library of Congress Catalog Card Number: 67–25881
First Published in West Germany © 1967 Herder KG
Printed in West Germany by Herder

CONTENTS

THE YEAR OF THE LORD

CONTENTS

THE YEAR OF THE LORD

The Judgment of the Son of Man

Luke 21:25–33

It is strange that the gospel read at the beginning of the time of preparation for Christmas is that of the end of the whole history of the world. Yet that is not really surprising. For what is afoot in a small beginning is best recognized by the magnitude of its end. What was really meant and actually happened by the coming, the "advent", of the redeemer is best gathered from that completion of his coming which we rather misleadingly call the "second coming". For in reality it is the fulfilment of his *one* coming which is still in progress at the present time.

For that reason, however, our Church advent is not a mere looking back to something past but is man's entrance by faith, hope and love into the process which began when God himself entered the history of his world and made it his own. As a result, that history is inexorably moving towards the day which today's gospel places prophetically before our eyes. From the picture of the fulfilment we are to gather what in reality is already happening in the depth of our life and our reality, though unobtrusively and quietly and therefore in a way which in our sinful blindness we may overlook. God has started on his way. He is already there, hidden, and the revelation of his being is at hand.

Now when it is manifest that he has come, we shall see him as the Son of man. As one of us. As one who has lived our life among us, just as it is, short, bitter, mysterious. It is as the Son of man that God will then question us about our life. In that judgment we shall not be able to say that he, the eternal in his infinite harmony, cannot after all enter into our life with sympathetic understanding of its fragility and unsolved enigmas. He not merely entered into it by sympathetic understanding, he literally lived it. He himself became flesh. Not the remote God but the Son of man will be the judgment or the justification of our lives. The man who is God will be our judgment. Because he is man, he knows just how it is with human beings. Yet he, the eternal, remote God, is as closely concerned about us as only a man can be who loves what is human and hates inhumanity in man from his own experience.

Is it more blessed or more dangerous to be judged by a man and not solely by a God who was not himself involved in the history he is judging? Who can say? At all events the gospel tells us the fact. The Son of man is to judge. If, however, the man who is God is to be our judgment, and if in his coming he travelled as we do from the womb of his Mother to the bosom of the earth, then the face of the Son of man, in which we shall one day read our judgment, already mysteriously gazes at us from every human face, because all are his brothers and sisters: the pure face of the child, the care-worn faces of the poor, the tear-stained faces of sinners, even the embittered faces of our so-called opponents and enemies. One day we shall have to "raise our heads" and look into the face of him who comes as the Son of man, for he is after all the God of eternity. And from his countenance all will look at us: all those around us through whom we were good or guilty. A voice will come from that mouth: What you did—or did not—do to the least of my brethren. That voice from that face will not die away and will fill our eternity from end to end. Shall we be able to raise our heads with the confidence of the forgiven and the living towards that face of the Son of man?

The Festival Time of Grace

Matthew 11:2–10

The Baptist stands in the advent period. He fits into *our* advent season. For isn't our life still Advent: faith, expectation, patience and longing for what is not yet visible? Do not we Christians have to build on what is "merely" hoped for and believed in? If we really want to be Christians, do we not, with God's folly, have to sacrifice the bird in the hand here on earth for the sake of the two in the heavenly bush—monetary advantage, pleasures of the body, harsh insistence on our rights, for the sake of the Kingdom of heaven, that Kingdom of heaven, alas, which no eye has seen?

The Baptist of today's gospel belongs to such an Advent of waiting for what is still to come. He was in reality what we ought to be in our lifelong season of Advent. He was in prison. He had been stupid enough to speak the truth even to the master of the State. How could anyone be as politically unrealistic as that? He sits there. It serves him right. No one gets him out. His friends do not start a revolt. They are much too insignificant for that, only interested in theology and quite ineffectual in real life, or so it seems at any rate. And God, too, leaves his preacher of penance where he is. He too seems to be on the side of the big battalions. And yet he was working miracles in his Son. But—is it

tragedy or comedy?—those miracles cured a few poor
wretches of apparently no great importance for the Kingdom of God. Those miracles did not free the holy prophet,
the blood relation and quite official precursor of the man
who was working the miracles. He remained imprisoned
until he was "liquidated".

It is not easy for a prophet to sit in prison waiting for
certain death, written off, and at the same time to take an
interest in miracles which are of no help to himself.

But the Baptist is not a reed shaken by the wind. He believes despite everything. He is the messenger preparing
the way for God, in his own life and heart first of all, preparing the way for the God who takes such an inhumanly
long time to come and does not even hurry when his prophet
is perishing, the God who always seems to arrive only when
it is too late. The Baptist knows that God always makes his
point, that he wins by losing, that he is living and gives life
by being put to death himself, that he is the future which
seems to have no future. In a word, the Baptist believes. It
was not easy for him. His heart was bitter and the sky over-
cast. The question in his heart has a rather agonized ring:
Are you he who is to come? But that question was nevertheless addressed to the right person, to God who is man.
In *prayer* we may show even a frightened heart to God, a
heart that can practically do no more and no longer knows
how long its strength will hold out. In a heart that prays
there still remains faith and this receives a sufficient answer:
"Go and tell John what you see . . . and blessed is he who
takes no offence at me" even if he sits abandoned in prison.

We are in Advent all through our lives, for we Christians
await one who is still to come. Only then shall we be proved
right. Until then, however, the world seems to be right. The
world will laugh, you will weep, our Lord said. We too are

sitting in a dungeon, in the prison of death, of unanswered questions, of our own weakness, our own meanness, of the hardship and tragedy of life. We shall not get out alive. But every day we shall send the messengers of our faith and prayer to him who will come thence to judge the living and the dead. These advent messengers will come back each time with the answer: I am coming; blessed is he who takes no offence at me.

Patience with the Provisional

John 1:19–28

Once again the Baptist stands before us in our advent longing and expectation. The question is put to him: What are
you really doing, if you are not the real, expected Messiah?
That is a language we can understand only too well. The
people of advent, of waiting for God, of burning longing
for the eternal, can be overcome by the most terrible
and dangerous impatience that there is, a religious radi-
calism which has the appearance of being glorious and
sublime but in reality is the contrary of the truly advent
attitude.

Man thirsts for God, hopes in him, hopes that he will soon
establish his Kingdom. He wills the unconditional, the
radiant truth whose splendour at once burns every doubt
from the mind, the radical goodness which would destroy
all fear that goodness itself is only a form of self-seeking.
But only precursors ever come; only beginnings are made;
messengers come but always with God's truth still in merely
human words which obscure it. Those messengers of God
are only men with human traits and sometimes inhuman
ones. All that ever happens are God's saving deeds (called
sacraments) in human ceremonies. All these provisional
things simply continue to proclaim that they themselves

are not the reality. The reality is merely hidden there in all those non-real words, human beings, signs.

Then man, who even in his purest religious feeling is a sinner, may lose patience. What are you doing in religion, you human beings, words, signs, if you are after all not the reality, not the unveiled God immediately present? Then the impatient think that this God may perhaps be found outside the human beings, the words and the signs of the Church: in nature, in the infinity of their own heart, in political projects to establish for ever by force here and now, the Kingdom of God. Or somewhere else. But in the end these impatient people realize, very often too late, that they have wandered into the wilderness of their own empty hearts where the devils dwell, not God; into the loveless desert of a blind and cruel nature which is only benevolent on Sunday afternoons; into the arid wasteland of the world where the waters of ideals ooze away the farther one advances; into the desolate wilderness of a politics which brings about not the Kingdom of God but simply the tyranny of naked force.

No, we are not spared it. We have to hear the voice of one crying in the wilderness, even if it confesses: It is not I. We must have the patience of men of advent. The Church is only the voice of one crying in the wilderness, announcing that the final radiant Kingdom of God is still coming and that when God wills, not when it suits us. We cannot try to ignore that voice simply because it comes from the mouths of men; we cannot disregard the messenger of the Church because he too is not worthy to loosen the shoelaces of the Lord whose forerunner he is, or because he cannot call down fire from heaven like Elijah. For it is still advent. The Church itself is still an advent Church; for we are still waiting for him who is to come in the unveiled radiance of unconditional

Godhead with the eternal Kingdom. And that Church rightly tells the impatient who want to see God directly here and now: Prepare for this God the true way, the way of faith, of love, of humility, and the way of patience with its unimpressive provisional messengers and their poor words and small signs. For then God will certainly come. He only comes to those who in patience love his forerunners and the provisional. The Pharisees of the gospel, however, who rejected the forerunner of the Messiah because he was not the definitive reality, did not recognize him who was the definitive reality either.

The Stumbling-Block of the History of Redemption

Luke 3: 1–6

The scandalous thing about Christianity, Christ himself and his Church will always be that they are historical. Precisely in the fifteenth year of the Emperor Tiberius, people think, precisely in Judaea and Galilee, precisely under the petty princes of those days, under a certain Pilate and under Annas and Caiaphas! Why did the salvation of all men not begin at the very beginning of all? Why not everywhere and always? Is the God of eternity, to whom all the world belongs, not equidistant from every place and time?

And yet it was then and there that the word of the Lord went forth to John and the decisive phase of the sacred history of redemption began. And so things have remained. People have to be baptized precisely with water, and nothing else will do. They have to have the word of forgiveness of sins spoken to them by a human mouth precisely on a Saturday afternoon in a wooden box—called a confessional—and not merely want to hear God's quiet voice in the voice of their own hearts. And the beauty of God's nature is not in fact the Church in which men find the body which once suffered on the Cross for us under Pontius Pilate. The words in the catechism and not the ideas in the empyrean of metaphysics are the truths by which people can live and die.

God himself can find man everywhere, where man inculpably and with a clear conscience cannot advance. And God in his mercy will do so liberally, without our having to arrange for it. But that does not prove that we can prescribe to him where we will be pleased to allow ourselves to be found by him. He can follow all ways; we, his creatures, only those which he has prescribed for us.

Now he *has* marked out certain definite ways of salvation for us. It is not the case that all our ways lead to God. He has marked out definite paths for us so that we may know and acknowledge that salvation is *his* grace, his free, gratuitous grace and not a right of our own, something he owes us. So that we may realize and acknowledge that he is not at our disposal but that we have to stand at his, that he is God and we his creatures. He has marked out definite ways of salvation for us because he himself—grace beyond all measure!—willed to walk them, because he himself willed to become a human being, caught like us in space and time and history from which in truth no human mind can extricate itself in this world. He himself was born under the Emperor Augustus, precisely in Nazareth from which no good can come, suffered under Pontius Pilate, imprisoned in the here and now, in the not-then and not-there of a real human being. Dear grace of a God who loves man. We do not need to seek God in his kingdom of infinity where after all we would hopelessly lose our way as though in a trackless void.

In fact Christianity is so human and so historical that it is too human for many people, who think that the true religion must be inhuman, i.e., not of the senses, non-historical. But the Word was made flesh. The word of the Lord went forth to John in the fifteenth year of the Emperor Tiberius. And so it has remained. Christianity is an historical and a very concrete and sturdy religion, a stumbling-block to the proud, who really—at least in religious matters—do not wish to be human beings, but it is grace and truth for those who with humble hearts are willing to be human beings in space and time even when they are adoring the God of eternity and infinity.

The Answer of Silence

Letter to a friend

Christmas? One says the word almost with despair, for can one really explain to anyone nowadays what it means to celebrate Christmas? It is obvious that the feast is not merely the Christmas tree, presents, family gatherings, and other emotionally appealing customs which are themselves only kept up with a certain scepticism. But what more is it? Let me attempt to give you something like a recipe.

The great experiences of life are of course one's destiny, a gift of God and of his grace, but they nevertheless mostly only fall to the lot of those who are prepared to receive them. Otherwise the star rises above a man's life but he is blind to it. For the sublime hours of wisdom, art and love, a man must prepare himself wholly with soul and body. So it is with the great days on which we celebrate our redemption. Do not leave them to chance; do not drift into them listlessly in an everyday frame of mind. Prepare yourself; determine to prepare yourself—that is the first thing.

Another thing. Have the courage to be alone. Only when you have really achieved that, when you have done it in a Christian way, can you hope to present a Christmas heart, that is, a gentle, patient, courageous, delicately affectionate heart, to those whom you are striving to love. That gift is the real Christmas-tree gift, otherwise all other presents are merely futile expense which can be indulged in at any time. First of all, then, persevere for a while on your own. Perhaps you can find a room where you can be on your own. Or you may know a quiet path or a lonely church.

Then do not talk to yourself the way you do with others, the people we argue and quarrel with even when they are not there. Wait, listen, without expecting any unusual experience. Do not pour yourself out in accusation, do not indulge yourself. Allow yourself to meet yourself in silence. Perhaps then you will have a terrible feeling. Perhaps you will realize how remote all the people are whom you are dealing with every day and to whom you are supposed to be bound by ties of love. Perhaps you will perceive nothing but a sinister feeling of emptiness and deadness.

Bear with yourself. You will discover how everything that emerges in such silence is surrounded by an indefinable distance, permeated as it were by something that resembles a void. Do not yet call it God! It is only what points to God and, by its namelessness and limitlessness, intimates to us that God is something other than one more thing added to those we usually have to deal with. It makes us aware of God's presence, if we are still and do not flee in terror from the mystery which is present and prevails in the silence—do not flee even to the Christmas-tree or to the more tangible religious concepts which can kill religion.

But that is only the beginning, only the preparation of a Christmas celebration for you. If you persevere in this way and, by keeping silence, allow God to speak, this silence which cries out is strangely ambiguous. It is both fear of death and the promise of the infinity which is close to you in benediction. And these are too close together and too similar for us to be able of ourselves to interpret this infinity which is remote and yet close. But precisely in this strangeness and mystery we learn to understand ourselves rightly and to accept the dear familiarity of this strange mystery. And that is precisely the message of Christmas: that in reality God is close to you, just where you are, if you are open to this infinity. For then God's remoteness is at the same time his unfathomable presence, pervading all things.

He is there with tender affection. He says: Do not be afraid. He is within, in the prison. Trust to this close presence, it is not emptiness. Cast off, and you will find. Relinquish and you are rich. For in your interior experience you are no longer dependent on what is tangible and solid, what by affirming itself isolates itself, what can be held fast. You have not merely things of that kind, for infinity has become presence. *That* is how you must interpret your interior experience and in that way know it as the high festival of the divine descent of eternity into time, of infinity into the finite, of God's marriage with his creature. Such a festival takes place in you—the theologians aridly call it "grace"; it takes place in you when you are still and wait and—believing, hoping and loving—interpret correctly, that is, in the light of Christmas, what it is you experience.

It is only this experience of the heart which brings proper understanding of the message of the Christmas faith: God has become man. Of course, we repeat that so easily. We think of the incarnation as though it were a sort of disguising of God, so that fundamentally God remains purely and simply God and we do not rightly know whether he is really here where we are. God is man—that does not mean he has ceased to be God in the measureless plenitude of his glory. Nor does it mean that what is human about him is something which does not really concern him and is only something assumed accessorily which says nothing really about him but only something about us. "God is man" really says something about God.

God's human nature must not be equated with God's divinity in total identity of kind nor yet simply be juxtaposed with God as a reality which perpetually relapses into its own mere identity. We must not link it with him merely verbally by an empty "and". If God shows this human nature of his, it always comes to us in such a way that *he himself* is there. Because we only juxtapose divinity and humanity in the incarnate Word of the Father, instead of understanding that they both spring from the one self-same ground, we are constantly in danger of missing each time the point where the blessed mystery of Christmas finds the place in our self-transcending human reality at which it fits into our life and our history as our salvation.

Do not forget that, as faith testifies, Jesus is true man, that is, one like you and me; a finite, free human being obediently accepting the unfathomable mystery of his being; one who must answer and does answer, who is questioned and hears the question, the question which is infinite and to which answer is only given in that ultimate act of the heart which surrenders itself lovingly and obediently to the infinite mystery, in an act in which acceptance takes place in virtue of the very reality which is accepted. That was the case also for him whose beginning you are going to celebrate. Because he accepted as a human being, you too can dare to do what he did: quietly and with faith to say "Father" to incomprehensibility, to accept it, not as deadly remoteness and consuming judgment on our wretchedness, but as measureless, merciful presence. For he is both God and man: giver, gift and reception, call and answer in one.

It would be good, then, if we were to call on the experience of our heart, in order to form some faint conception of what is meant by the incarnation of the eternal God. It would be well if this were to be done in that silence in which alone we are present to ourselves in self-awareness. Such silence, correctly understood in faith in the Christmas message, is an experience of what is infinite in man's reality, an experience of man's being which tells us something which is only so because God himself became man. We would experience ourselves differently if God had not been born man.

If we accept the silent tremendous reality which surrounds us like remote distance, yet close and overwhelming, if we accept it as saving presence and a tender unreserved love; if we have the courage to understand ourselves in a way which can only be done in grace and faith—whether this is realized or not—then we have had the Christmas experience of grace in faith. It is very simple but it is the peace which is promised in their goodwill to the men of God's good pleasure.

The Great Joy

Let us keep Christmas, a festival of faith and of love for the Word who became flesh, a festival also of love for one another because man can love man since God himself became man. Let us worship God because he loved man and his poor flesh so much that he placed it imperishably for all eternity in the very midst of the blazing flame of his Godhead. Incomprehensible God, adventurer of love! We had thought that man, pitiable as he is, could only be a primitive, unsuccessful trial-model for the superman who has still to come; it is hard for us to bear with ourselves—and especially with others—just as we are. Not unreasonably, for man is difficult to endure, for he is a continual failure and falls from one extreme to another.

And yet, as the Church sings in its noblest hymn, he did not disdain the Virgin's womb. He himself came into his creation, into humanity. If it were not for this fact of facts, would we have the courage to believe that God was successful with his work? He himself has entered into all the narrow limits of man which it would seem could only exist at an infinite distance from him: his mother's body, a small defeated native country under foreign occupation, a desperate state of the age, a narrow-minded milieu, unsuccessful

politics, a body marked out for death, the prison of in-
comprehension, the monotony of the working day, of
complete failure, the dark night of abandonment by God
and of death. He spared himself nothing. The narrow
confines, however, into which God himself has entered,
must have an issue. It must be worthwhile being a human
being, if God was not satisfied to be in himself but also
willed in addition to be one of these human beings, and if
that was not too dangerous or too trivial for him. Mankind
is not a herd, but a sacred family, if God himself is a member
of it as a brother. The tragedy of its history must after
all have a blessed outcome, if God does not just observe
this hardly divine comedy unmoved from the throne
of his infinity but takes part in it himself, as seriously as
all the rest of us, who have to do so whether we want to
or not.

The so-called "genuine reality" both of the embittered
and disillusioned and of the superficial "bon vivant" is
reduced to a mere semblance which only unbelieving fools
take in deadly earnest or with greedy seriousness, now that
God himself has become the true reality behind and in the
midst of this appearance. Eternity is already in the heart of
time, life is at the centre of death, truth is stronger than lies,
love more powerful than hatred, the wickedness of man already irrevocably conquered by God's grace. Christianity
is indeed an optimism about man such as only God could
conceive. It is not surprising that it seems so unlikely to us.
There is no need for the superman if God himself became
man. Mere humanism is long since obsolete if in the Son of
the Father and of the Virgin man is to become God, as the
Fathers say, if man is infinitely more than man. Man can be
exacting; in fact, properly understood, he can never be
demanding enough in regard to God; there is only one

thing which he may not do: will to be less than the brother
of the eternal Word of the Father who became flesh.

Up, then, and let us be kind at least on this day and this
holy night. Perhaps we shall then see that it is not really so
difficult, and then we shall also contrive to be so in the New
Year too. Let us be kind! We have no right to demand a
better world if we do not begin the improvement ourselves
in our own heart. Let us be kind today! After all we do not
have to be malicious and bitter and defend ourselves greedily
and anxiously against others. God has come. No one can
take him from us and he is everything. He is our brother.
So it is right to bear in our own heart our brother's love of
humanity and his kindness, to be gentle and forgiving,
hopeful, serene and cheerful, unsuspicious and loyal. God
himself has tried this and has told us that it works. His experience is more decisive and credible than ours: we can
be better than we think. More can be made of us than we
suspect. If Christ is formed in us, we can never form too
high a conception of ourselves. We are more than we can
imagine.

So let us sing with the gaiety of a heart which is set free for
God's eternal youth. The darkness has become bright. God
himself has prepared a festival for himself which did not
exist before in his heaven: he has become man. Heaven and
earth ring out in God's silent, holy night which is lighter
than the gloomy day of men: Glory to God, peace to man
in whom God was so well-pleased. Let us fall on our knees
and joyfully read the Gospel: At that time a decree went
forth from the Emperor Augustus . . .

Holy Night

Why do we call the feast we are keeping today a "sacred night"? Historically speaking, of course, we do not know for certain that Jesus was born at night. The account of the shepherds who were keeping the night-watches over their flocks and heard the heavenly message of the Saviour's birth is not of course in itself a conclusive proof that Jesus himself was born at night. And yet Christendom has always thought of this blessed birth of the redeemer as taking place at night. The German language has even incorporated this conviction into the name it gives the feast—Weih-nacht: sacred night. Why?

Night for man has two aspects. Like almost all the factors in human existence, it has a double meaning, is ambiguous. Night can be something uncanny and sombre, the time when no man can work, as Jesus says in scripture; it is felt as akin to death; it is the time of what is undefined, uncertain and dangerous, of what is obscure and impalpable. Consequently in the religious domain night can have this symbolic meaning. In scripture "night" stands for the time of unbelief and sin, the time of judgment and divine visitation. Therefore the Christians must be children of the day, they must shine like stars in the night so that they are not taken by surprise

by the judge who comes like a thief in the night. Consequently we must watch, we may not sleep, we must rise from sleep
and walk as though in the day-time. But for human sensibility, even as this finds expression in scripture, night has yet
another aspect. It is the time of silence and concentrated
strength, self-contained, ready to wait and allow things to
mature. It is in the middle of the night that the cry is heard
that the bridegroom is coming. Night in scripture is the
time of heavenly dreams. Because night is the time of
liberation from the enslaving impressions and ties of superficial everyday routine, it is a time of prayer, and so Jesus
spends whole nights in converse with God. The night can
be affectionately regarded as God's creature, so that the
psalmist (74:16) can pray: "Thine is the day and thine is the
night." And Daniel (3:71) summons the night to praise God,
just as of course, according to the psalmist, every night
hands on to the next the message of the glory of God, for
already in the psalm (19:3), the heavens by their silent
grandeur and immeasurable vastness speak to the pious
mind of God's greatness.

Why can we feel about the night in such different ways?
We experience it as a beginning, as something still indefinite,
which has still to be followed by what is really meant and
decisive: the light of day. Beginning and possibility, however, are ambiguous; a good promise which is not yet
fulfilled, a vast, free possibility which has not yet found its
realization, the plan which is splendid but has not yet been
carried out. All that is necessarily ambiguous: promising
and threatened and threatening at one and the same time,
something provisional which may still set off for distant
goals but which is still uncertain of arriving.

Now if there is a moment in history, the history of the
individual and of mankind, which resembles an absolutely

first beginning, full of incalculable possibilities and promise, a beginning which conceals everything mysteriously within it, and if this starting-point of an ineffable, infinite beginning even bears within it the certainty of its own realization, is already sure of its triumph, is already as much fulfilment as promise, then that moment would deserve to be called the holy night. Night, because a beginning, holy night because a blessed and unconquerable beginning; of such a beginning we would have to say: holy night, sacred night. And so we sing: "Silent night, holy night". Everywhere in the world these words are sung for this feast. And it was not by chance that in the fourth century this feast was placed at the season when in nature too the sun as it were begins its course anew. At that time they fixed the beginning of the "sun of justice" as the prophet calls our Saviour, on the day of the pagan "natalis solis invicti", the festival of the birth of the "unconquered sun-god".

With a sacred right. For this hour *is* the holy and sacred night. Faith tells the Christians: That was the beginning. There God himself came gently forth from the terrifying radiance in which he dwells as God and Lord, and came to us; he quietly entered the poor dwelling of our earthly existence and was found as a man; he began where we begin, quite poor, vulnerable, quite childlike and gentle, quite helpless. He who is the infinite, distant future which of ourselves we never reach because it seems to retreat farther and farther away as we hurry towards it on the hard roads of life, he himself has approached us, arrived among us, because otherwise we should never have found our way to him. He has accompanied us on our way to him so that this may find a blessed end, because the very end itself has become our beginning. God is near; his eternal word of mercy is where we are; it is a pilgrim on our paths, experiences our

joy and our distress, lives our life and dies our death. He has
brought his eternal life quietly and gently into this world
and its death. He has redeemed us, for he shared our lot. He
made our beginning his own, followed the path of our
destiny and so opened it up into the infinite expanses of God.
And because he accepted us irrevocably, because God's
Word will never cease to be man, this beginning which is
ours and his is a beginning of indestructible promises, and
his silent beginning by night is a holy and sacred night.

This also shows how we must celebrate Christmas. As
the mystery of the holy night. Our heart must be quiet,
recollected and gentle, unreservedly open like the heart of a
child which does not yet shut itself to any of the possibilities
of its existence but is unsuspectingly ready for them all.
What is in the background of our being, its breadth and
range beyond our control, must silently prevail in us, just
as the night—by causing what is manageable and measurable
to fade—brings the far distance close, without narrowing it.
We must dare to admit this nocturnal silence into our interior
selves, by abandoning that flight into business, chatter and
fuss by which we try to run away from ourselves and the
mystery above us because, unaccustomed to it, we are
frightened even by the great mystery of infinite love. We
ought not to profane the sacred night on which our life too
was hallowed, by festivities which are too facile. The
familiar, childlike character of this feast which is of course
quite appropriate to such a day, ought nevertheless to
remain transparent to the ineffable mystery which alone
makes men profoundly familiar with one another and gives
them the promise of eternal youth. Christmas is celebrated,
as it must be, if it is not to degenerate into a purely secular
festival, only by those who allow to recede in the silence of
the sacred night of quiet detachment and submissive devo-

tion in their own hearts that multiplicity of things, men and endeavours which at other times cloud the view of infinity. Sometimes, at least for a little while, they extinguish the earthly lights which usually hide the stars of heaven, and allow themselves to be addressed by the unutterable, wordless presence of God which speaks by its own silence, if we have ears for it. We should feel as we do on a clear winter's night when we go out under the starry sky; the light of human presence and of the safety of home still follows us, but above us is the sky and we are conscious of the silence of the night, which at other times may appear to us sinister and terrifying, as the quiet presence of the infinite mystery of our existence, which is both saving love and immeasurable grandeur.

It is the holy night of Christmas! The eternal future has entered our time. Its radiance still dazzles us, so that we think it is night. But at all events it is a blessed night, a night in which there is already warmth and light, which is beautiful, welcoming and secure by reason of the eternal day which it bears hidden within it. It is a silent, holy night for us, however, only if we admit the holy silence of this night into our inner selves, only if our heart too keeps watch in solitude. It can do so easily. For such solitude and quiet is not hard. The only difficulty about it is that of all lofty things which are simple and great. For of course we *are* solitary. There exists in our heart an interior land where we are alone, to which no one finds his way but God. This innermost, unfrequented chamber of our heart is really there—the only question is whether we ourselves avoid it foolishly out of guilty fear, because no one and no familiar things of this earth can accompany us if we enter it. Let us enter it quietly and shut the door behind us. Let us listen to the unutterable melody which sounds in the silence of that night.

The silent and solitary soul sings here to the God of the heart its quietest and most ardent song. And it can have confidence that he hears it. For this song no longer has to seek a beloved God beyond the stars in that inaccessible light in which he dwells and which makes him invisible to all. Because of Christmas, because the Word was made flesh, God is near and the quietest word in the stillest room of the heart, the word of love, comes to his ear and his heart. And those who have entered into themselves even when it is night, hear in this nocturnal quiet in the depth of the heart God's gentle word of love. One must be calm, not afraid of the night, hold one's peace. Otherwise we hear nothing. For the ultimate is only spoken in the silence of the night, now that in our night of life, through the gracious coming of the Word, there has come to be Christmas, holy night, silent night.

Grace in the Abysses of Man

It is no easy matter to write a commentary or something like a leading article for Christmas. The hearer or reader will have the same feeling. Every year it is the same thing: a certain amount of "Christmas spirit", a few pious and humanitarian phrases, a few expensive presents and the trouble of having to say thank you for them afterwards. And then everything goes on as before. If one is a Christian, one very definitely has the duty of not being under any illusions about this magical Christmas spirit. For a Christian cannot be a person who hides the pitiful reality of human life under pious phrases. By God, he cannot. For doesn't the Christian hang up on the walls which enclose his life, as a sign of his faith, a cross, a gibbet on which a man is nailed and dying? For him, then, Christmas can only mean the beginning of the life which in this world ends on this cross—or in death or the empty bitterness of total disappointment—it all amounts to the same thing.

After Christmas—this must be said at Christmas—everything goes on as before. We carry on as before. We go forward wonderfully well—to the moon or even farther. And finally to death, but for a respectable person of East or West it is best not to talk about that, because it isn't done, unless of course one is making an existentialist commotion about it, for there is money in that.

Is one angrily to make off somewhere during these days, then, or calmly to take part in "Christmas" because it is still best, still the most respectable thing, not to show one's innermost feelings? It would be possible, of course, instead of either of these, to do something else. One could in fact consider what Christmas actually means if it is understood in a Christian sense. An answer to that question might be of interest to the non-Christian as well. One might even ask oneself whether after all in one's heart of hearts, officially Christian or not, the unlikely courage to believe in Christmas, the real Christmas is actually in fact present after all. And this quite apart from whether one admits it or thinks oneself unable to believe.

God made Christmas without consulting us. It follows that it is in fact possible that we believe more than we admit, more than we know in our theoretical opinions about ourselves and our life. How is this? We human beings are of such a kind that we are always beyond and above ourselves. It is our burden and our dignity. We are free and responsible for ourselves; we are those who hope. We are always already beyond and above what can be mentioned, designated and specified. We live the tangible on the basis of the intangible. We are grounded in the abyss of what cannot be named or expressed. We can certainly, of course, shut ourselves off and say we can make nothing of it. We can try to stick to what is commonplace and within range, to inspect what light falls on and refuse to turn to the unfathomable light which alone makes visible for us what it shines on. Yet even so mystery permeates our human existence and compels us again and again to turn our eyes towards it: in the joy which has no longer an object, in the anguish which ends the obvious matter-of-factness of our existence, in the love which knows itself unconditional and eternally binding, in the question which takes fright at its own unconditionality and unlimited scope.

In this way we are always finding ourselves facing a mystery which is, which is without limit, which grounds without itself having a ground, which is always there and always withdraws, intangible. We call it God. We point to mystery as such when we say God. When we do not overlook thought because of what is thought of, joy because of what gives joy, responsibility because of what we take responsibility for, unending future because of the present, immeasurable hope because of the object of striving here and now, we are already concerned with God, whether we give to this namelessness this or that name or no name at all.

And if in the depth of our being we have accepted this thinking, loving, hoping human reality despite all the overhasty, impatient smarts and protests on the surface of our existence, then we have by that very fact entered into relations with God, given ourselves over to him. Many will do this even if they think that they do not know God (he must of course always be known as incomprehensible, otherwise something else has been mistaken for him), even if in their mute reverence they do not venture to name him.

In such acceptance of human existence, obediently entrusting itself to mystery, it is possible for what in Christian terminology is called grace to occur: God is mystery, and remains so. But he is the abyss in which the existence of man is accepted, he is presence and not simply remoteness, forgiveness and not simply judgment. He fills the unending question of thought, the immeasurable scope of hope and the infinite demand of love with himself, silent still and in that ground of our being which only opens out to us if we obediently allow ourselves to be encompassed by this mystery, without seeking to master it. If this happens, however, Christmas is already within us, that coming of God which Christianity acknowledges always to occur by the grace of God in every human being who does not refuse it by that guilt which is both terror of God and proud self-sufficiency.

But we are men of history, of the tangible here and now. And this coming of God, his action in us, was intended to be tangible and irrevocable, irrevocably and tangibly historical both as God's self-giving and as God's coming definitively accepted by man. Consequently mankind has experienced in human history this coming of God as definitive, unsurpassable and irrevocable. In Jesus of Nazareth. In him surrender to the infinite mystery as such is present as man's action. And this itself, like everything that involves freedom and decision, is grace. In him, God as ineffable mystery (and remaining so) has expressed himself as Word wholly and irrevocably. In him that Word is "there" as spoken to all of us, as the God of inexpressibly close presence and forgiveness.

Here question and answer, unmixed and inseparable, have become one. The one person is there in whom God and man are one, without detriment to one or the other.

Even when someone who is still far from any explicit and verbally formulated revelation accepts his human reality in silent patience, or rather in faith, hope and love (however he may name these), as a mystery which loses itself in the mystery of eternal love and bears life in the very midst of death, that person says Yes to Jesus Christ even if he does not realize it. For if someone lets go and jumps, he falls into the depth which is actually there, not merely the depth he has measured. Anyone who accepts his human reality—that is indescribably difficult and it remains uncertain whether we really do so—has accepted the Son of man, because in him God accepted man.

We read in scripture that those who love their neighbour have fulfilled the law. This is the ultimate truth because God himself has become that neighbour, and so in every neighbour it is always he, one who is nearest and most distant, who is accepted and loved. If we accept the silent mystery which encompasses our existence and surrounds us as what is remote and yet overwhelmingly close, if we accept it as saving presence and tender love given without reserve, if we have the courage to understand ourselves in this way, which can only be done in grace and faith, if we recognize the ground of this presence and its absolute promise and advent in him whom we call the God-man, then we have made the Christmas experience of grace in faith.

If in this way some have courage explicitly to believe in the truth of Christmas, if the others silently accept the unfathomable depth of their human reality which is namelessly filled with joyful hope and are themselves accepted by the first as "anonymous" Christians, then all can celebrate Christmas together. The apparently superficial and conventional business of Christmas then acquires truth and depth after all. The apparent falsehood of the whole business is then not the ultimate truth about it. Behind it stands the holy and silent truth that God has in fact come and celebrates Christmas with us.

So we are more honest, more profoundly true, if we go beyond an initial, only too justified scepticism in regard to ordinary conventional Christmas, and celebrate it candidly without taking our own scepticism seriously, as the sign that God's advent among us long ago outstripped all our plans and all our disappointments. Then if after Christmas things go on as before, it nevertheless remains true that God has accepted us. And the abysses within us are filled with his grace.

God's Coming into a Closed World

The feast of St Stephen

Today on the second day of Christmas the Church's liturgy celebrates the feast of St Stephen the deacon and first martyr of the original Church of Jerusalem, who was stoned to death soon after 35 A.D., that is, shortly after Jesus' death and resurrection. We read of him in the 6th and 7th chapters of the Acts of the Apostles. The reason why his feast is celebrated on this day is that the liturgical celebration of his death in the East was already fixed on the 26th December at a time in the 4th century when the Western Christmas of the 25th December was not yet established in the East. So Stephen did not come to the Crib, the Crib came to him. The feast of Stephen came from the East into Western Europe in the 5th century when it was already linked with Christmas.

It is only by historical accident that St Stephen's feast falls at Christmas. There was no "ideological" intention behind it. But of course contingent historical facts often have a profound meaning, and even make better sense than things rationally worked out and devised. And so the young hero with his palm can continue to stand by the Crib of the child on the straw. He fits in very well. For if we reflect what, according to scripture, Stephen's character and death have to tell us, we can see that it is definitely a Christmas message, providing we do not misunderstand Christmas itself.

He is a man of faith and of the Holy Spirit (6:5), of grace and strength (6:8). For that reason he is a man with freedom, or we might say with courage to move, to step out from merely inherited things and the secure fence of the mere letter of the law. And so, scripture tells us he foretells the destruction of the Temple, and in a completely Pauline way, even before Paul, he is aware of the supersession of the legal institutional aspect of the Old Testament by Jesus (6:14). Accordingly, in his speech in Chapter 7 of Acts he sees the whole history of the redemption and ruin of his nation as a single journey, a continual setting out, a move abroad, a repeated call and summons, a mission. The call comes from infinite mystery and summons to it. It is not a tangible idol which men themselves have made and carry ahead as a deceptive goal guiding their movement. Because he is perceptive in this way, Stephen himself is open to faith in that future of his people which he experiences in his own time, the coming of the Messiah, and so for the message of Christmas. Because of this perception he must summarize and interpret the history of perdition, which runs parallel to the redemptive history of open movement, as resistance to the prophets "who announced beforehand the coming of the Righteous One", as a resistance culminating in the treacherous death of him who is the goal of this movement (7:52f.). And when Stephen dies, he dies into what is opening out into the infinite limitlessness of his grace-given spiritual existence. Precisely at this limitless end he sees the one who came close in order to bring infinite distance close, who came to make the world itself in its totality God's place, who puts an end to idolatry of the world and its powers because he himself is the presence of God made man among us: "I see the heavens opened, and the Son of man standing at the right hand of God" (7:56).

And so the youth with the palm of victory by the Crib of the child is surely a good interpreter of Christmas. Christmas is God's coming into the closed world so that it may become open to God and heaven open for the world. Christmas means the world's journey has reached its goal because the destination of this perpetually renewed searching movement of history has been attained; but this end is the opening out of the world into God's own life which only now is brought about. We, alas, set before us the idols of our utopias and think we can move towards them as a goal. But we once again find in them our own aimlessness, futility and finitude which pass away and disintegrate. As Stephen preached, we make gods for ourselves which go before us (7:40). They move before us because we hold them out in front of us, for once again we project our problematic selves on the wall of the gloomy void towards which we are moving. Of course we could not accept a goal if we were not to attain ourselves in it. Yet how could we regard a goal as valid if we were only to find ourselves in it? What is to be done then? We wish to find ourselves and yet we cannot be satisfied with ourselves. We must have both ourselves and infinity, both together. If we call ourselves man and infinity God, then we can say what our goal would have to be, if it exists: the God-man. Christmas, however, actually says that the goal has come from God, and it is seeker and what is endlessly sought in one person: the Son of man, the God-man, the glory of God of which a glimpse can now be caught, but only if Jesus is seen standing at the right hand of God. The goal itself has approached the seeker and brought the seeker himself into what is sought so that he does not lose himself when he seeks what is wholly other. One finds

purely and simply by seeking, if one seeks with willingness
to be found by God and does not merely indulge oneself in
the rambling aimlessness of a movement which is not really
a search. Those who see pure openness and do not confuse
it with any concrete form, who are ready to take the here-
and-now and the everywhere-and-always as identical, and
to do so not merely as an abstract postulate which commits
one to nothing but in the concrete details of life; those who
in this way and for this reason find the only person in the
history of humanity whom it is possible to take to be this
unity of God and man: Jesus Christ,—these in their search
succeed in finding, in their unending movement arrive, not
because the two are identical from man's side, but because
God himself has found the seeker. If we accept ourselves
totally as we really are, as we are through the fact that the
Word of God himself has become flesh and out of our
darkness made Christmas, then we find what we seek. Then
the heavens are open for us in a Christmas way as they were
for Stephen, and in faith we see the glory of God, because
we see the one Son of man in triumph, the infinite man.
Truly, since Christmas came into existence the heavens are
open, because the heavens have come onto the earth. The
believer sees God who gazes at him in a human face and
loves him with a human heart. Since then the infinite is close
and the finite opens out onto infinite expanses.

NEW YEAR'S EVE AND NEW YEAR'S DAY

Spiritual Balance-Sheet of a Year

This is the last day of a year, so it is appropriate for us to take leave of the year in a Christian way. Each in the depth of his heart must take his leave of himself for himself. For each human being is different from the next. Every year that someone has lived through is therefore different from that of any other. God leads each by his own path. And in his infinity, in the incalculable plenitude of the possibilities which he contains within him and which as the creator and Lord of our life he can distribute, he is not a God who is compelled to treat two people precisely alike, even once, as though, so to speak, he could not think of anything different.

And yet the year of each human being in another sense is precisely the same as that of his neighbour and of everyone else. For it is past. That at least is common to them all. We are taking leave of the past year. We are doing it together in our churches in the community of the one body of grace. We are leaving a year behind us with its many days, its work, its cares, its disappointments, its bitternesses, with the plans we have had and which have perhaps come entirely to nothing or have only partly been realized. We are leaving it behind with our guilt, our failure, in fact with everything that our niggardly heart has made of the year.

To whom are we to give this year of which we are taking leave, which we are leaving behind? Is it still possible for us to give it to anyone? Is it not simply gone, inexistent? Is it not obliterated, departed, by the mere fact that we are taking leave of it and that it is no longer within the range of our possibilities of decision in the way it once was, when it was lived through, day by day and hour by hour? On the contrary, if we see it in a Christian way, if we take God into account, if we recognize ourselves for what we are, spiritual beings of eternity, we must in fact say that the past year is the year which has been gained, retained, the irrevocable, enduring year. The years which we have lived through are our years. Whether the coming years will also be our years, God knows, we do not. The past is ours, as Christians we can calmly say this, and we can hope and wish that God will give us a long future in this life, this finite life, and that this too will become our own by enduring even while it appears to pass away.

Who preserves the past, enduring, irrevocable year for us? God. He has entered it in what scripture calls the "book of life". He knows it, and in his sight it remains present. He has inscribed it in the "book of life" which is what we ourselves are in our spiritual substance, in the historical spiritual characteristics which we ourselves in our life and therefore during the past year also, have indelibly stamped in that spiritual substance which is ourselves. Because in this way this year is still there, in an hour of farewell such as this, we can still make of it what it ought to be.

Let us bid farewell to the old year thankfully so that it may become what it ought to be, the gift of the grace of God. For God has given us all the days of this year. And if we have truly accepted them as gifts of his love—and it is always within our power to do this—they have been blessed days, days of grace and salvation. We must never think of ourselves so sullenly, wearily, sceptically or morosely that this brooding actually becomes a mistrustful way of thinking about God himself. If we were only to say that we have been poor, failures, burdened, weary, afraid, that we have been adequate neither to our life nor to God's call, then we would perhaps have said something true. But if as Christians we were to say no more than this about ourselves and our past year, we should be unjust to God. Has he not preserved us in his grace? Has he not repeatedly given us the blessed Body of his Son? Isn't his Holy Spirit in our hearts? Have we not after all borne God's burden through the year, though perhaps only with difficulty and groaning under it? Has God's grace not done good to others even through us? For that matter we cannot say that the good that we did not find difficult to do was no true goodness in the eyes of God; and it is not even necessarily true that we have often or mostly omitted the good which we found difficult, except when it was forced from us by God through the hardships of life. Have we not resigned ourselves even after some grumbling and protest to much that we found hard, and accepted it? And that means, even if we do not very explicitly realize it, that we have accepted God, because it is only possible calmly to accept what is deadly by reaching out to true unlimited life. If we had not done that we should not now, on the last evening of the year, have come before the face of God at all, and in that case we should certainly not be able to look back on this year, and could not bless it.

But because by God's grace it was what it was as we lived through it, because despite everything it was more God's gracious deed in us than our failure, we can bless it, we must and may do so. We can take leave of this year gratefully and entrust it to the grace and love of God, the love of the God who is eternity and who preserves for us for our eternity what we are taking our leave of today and tomorrow. What we give in gratitude, God receives in grace, and what is so accepted by him is redeemed and made holy, blessed and set free. And so it remains for eternity: a year of ours which is saved and acquired for ever.

And then we go on and we take with us from this past year our old selves with the old tasks, the old cares, the old burdens and anxieties, the old fear which stands somewhere in our souls too, with the feeling of being poor and of having to ask every day for bread and for strength to endure at least for a day.

But even if now as we are taking our leave of the old year, we are not yet looking forward into the new, we can nevertheless take ourselves heartened into the new year. Even just as we are, for simply like that we are the creatures of God the eternal Father, the work of his hands. He made us. He takes responsibility for what he has made. He answers for world history and the life of each one of us. He has encompassed us with his goodness, his love and fidelity. If we take with us into the new year the burden of our past, ourselves with all our cares, with all our weakness and weariness, God, faithful and good, goes with us. And the burden which we go on carrying into the new year is not greater than we can bear. Even if it were to crush us, God would receive us into his own blessed happiness. And what seemed the ultimate pain and the ultimate torment, in reality would simply be relief from all burdens and entry into God's incomprehensible life.

We do not bear more than we are able to bear. If we have

the impression that what was light and joyous in the old year remains behind and its burden comes with us, let us say as we take leave of the old year: "My God, you are coming with me and so I will gladly take with me from the old year everything which I cannot simply leave behind as yours, for you to preserve for me as my eternal life."

So let us bid farewell to the past year. It was a year of the Lord, a year of his grace, even a year of growth in the interior life, even if we did not perceive this, because it is in our weakness that God's strength must triumph. And so at the end of the year we can all truly praise God and thank and glorify him, for he is good and his mercy endures for ever.

In the Name of Jesus

Luke 2:21

We are beginning a new year in secular life, not a new Church year. But the earthly year, everyday life, the life of work and worry, is of course the field in which our salvation has to be worked out in God's sight. And so we have every reason to begin this year too in God's name. Let us in God's name then begin once more, go on once more, honestly and unwearied. Time presses. One can fall into despair or melancholy when one realizes on New Year's Eve that yet another part of one's earthly life is irrevocably past. But time presses on towards God and eternity, not towards the past and destruction. And so—in God's name!

There is a pious custom of writing C + M + B above the doors at Epiphany. Let us inscribe above the gate of the New Year the name of God, the name of the God in whom is our help, the name of Jesus. Jesus means: Yahweh helps. Yahweh was the proper name of the God of the Old Testament nation of the Covenant. That we can give God a name, God the nameless and incomprehensible, whom man of himself ultimately knows only as remote and obscure and incomprehensible, is due to the fact that he made himself known in the history of his own action and speech. We can perceive from the way in which he acts how he really wills to be in our regard. All the experiences which man has had with the living God in his action in us are summed up in the "name" of his God. Only a proper name, never a merely abstract general concept, comprises the full, indivisible and irreducible totality of what can be experienced of a living person through lasting relations with them. And Jesus as a proper name tells us how Yahweh willed to be in our regard: close, loving, helpful, faithful to the end. In Jesus and by him we know what we have in God. Otherwise we do not. He is the Word of the Father, in whom as the word of mercy God expresses himself to the world. Consequently if we wish to say who our God is, we must say "Jesus". If we were to forget this Word, God would disappear for us into the dark inaccessibility of an incomprehensible "ground of the world". But we Christians know the definitive name of God: Jesus. For that is the name which that child received who is God and the eternal youth of the world, who is a man and as such the eternal countenance of God. Let us give this name to the coming year. Let us sign the Cross of this Jesus on brow, mind and heart. Let us say with relief: our help is in the name of the Lord! And then stout-heartedly let us cross the threshold of the New Year. If his name shines above it, even its darkest hour will be an hour of the year of the Lord and of his salvation.

A new year is coming. What will it bring? I do not mean for the world, for politics and the Church. I mean, for me. Precisely for me. This question and this concern are justified. For one day I shall depart, I shall no longer be here. And it is my faith, not my egotistical imagination which tells me that then I shall really exist, that I am what I have become here and now, that the yield of this time here is gathered in what we call eternity, mine and yours, unique, inexchangeable, untransferable. And so I have a right to ask what the new year will bring me. And all other history is ultimately only important (though it is so to a degree which superficial people are far from realizing) for what it brings for this and that person, for you and me in that eternity. For all else passes and is not very important because it is soon over. It is possible, of course, to say that this transitory reality, rightly understood, is itself eternity in process of becoming; the eternal being the temporal brought to perfect fulfilment, not something coming afterwards in a temporal sense, for otherwise this would pass away in its turn. And so I am interested in what the new year will bring. I am interested in it with the whole seriousness of eternity. For what is coming will not depart. It is coming to stay. It occurs in order to be, not to pass away. It plunges into the void of time in order to fill it. It is the mystery of eternity in time. It is impossible for me to take what the new year brings as seriously as it needs to be. For as long as I am passing with my human reality through time as it flows away, I always think it contains nothing but itself. I have perpetually to rouse myself. What is eternal is happening in me now, once and for all, now when I think that what is passing and passing away is not very important.

Not all my moments are equally full of this happening which abides. When would a moment of my time be "fulfilled", as we speak of the "fullness" of time which came for the world as a whole with the incarnate Word of God? Evidently it would occur if a moment came in which, with complete awareness, courage and determination, I had concentrated myself completely and, having collected myself entirely and comprised myself in my freedom, I gave myself wholly to God, quite unselfishly, in that indescribable way which we call love of God, of God whom we only really know if we achieve that indescribable thing. And this would not be with sentimental, unctuous familiarity, but with stern severity and silent fidelity, for God is incomprehensible. I should then possess myself only in such a way that my self-possession would be an act of perfect self-giving and dispossession. And all that is meant, of course, as a Christian act. For whether one realizes this or not, the occurrence of such an act, in the present order of things, is faith and grace. The God in question can only be reached because he himself, while remaining infinite, has come close to us (whether this is known or not) in Christ Jesus. He is the word of love which God has spoken into our world in such a way that it can be heard where otherwise we would hear nothing but the silence of God, and we do not know whether that is a blessed word of love or implies eternal damnation. But when does such an act take place in me? When do I concentrate myself wholly and in entire freedom give myself to God? It is of course right, praiseworthy and good to say (but it ought not to set us too much at ease) that we think of God, we mean well, keep his commandments, and therefore (so we think) nothing can really happen to us; he must be gracious to us; he must reward us (as we Catholics say), at least he must pardon us (as many others say). All that may of course be true. Indeed it is true, but not the whole truth which I am concerned with here. After all we have to love God with our whole heart, with all our strength, with our whole soul. And yet that has to be done while we are still on pilgrimage far from the Lord, while we still do not see him face to face. For the promised blessedness is only to be the final, abiding perfect completion of time, of love in time.

We must therefore have given ourselves totally to him in the freedom of this time, in order totally to attain him. It cannot be done for less. No quarter is given. And all grace consists in his bestowing on us the gift of doing this. It does not consist of his giving beatitude without our doing it ourselves (in time as eternity). Even the poor crucified thief was heard in such a way that in his last hour he began to believe and to love with his whole heart, with all his strength and with his whole soul. But when does this happen with me? Where is God's grace totally victorious in the total freedom in which the cowardly and frightened creature who elsewhere will not abandon self, finds the courage to take the plunge, really to forget self completely for the sake of God? Where and when shall I achieve that? I must already have contrived to, I may tell myself encouragingly. For, of course, I trust that I am living in God's grace, that I have found his mercy and his Holy Spirit which is poured out in our hearts as love of God. And so (it may be said) the situation is not so dangerous and terrifyingly improbable in regard to that total love of God, without attaining which no one can definitively find his God. Can we say, it may be asked (in order to have to ask less anxiously), that one must somewhere and somehow love God in the centre of the person, really genuinely and honestly, but one does not need to have yet comprised one's whole life in this total love of God "now", at the moment when we are anxiously framing the question. For by asking it, we show that we are still journeying, still in the historical course of human existence. And for that very reason we do not yet have to be finished, because as an historical being one cannot yet be finished. The course has to be run, it may be said. It is not permitted deliberately to stand still, benumbed; we have to will to go on, to grow in this love. And if one does this, the argument runs, then even now everything is as it should be, even now when we do not yet find a totally all-transforming love in ourselves, covetous and selfish as we are, though believing and of good will; we have charity and it will grow, if we do not deliberately waste the opportunities offered by life and the grace of God.

Once again, all that may be correct. In fact it is correct, and that is a consolation. But it is not complete consolation, for, even so, somewhere or other in my life the moment of the fullness of time must nevertheless occur. That one, comprehensive, great and holy event must occur, the moment, still and silent like a Christmas night, in which a man's heart gives him so wholly into the hands of the incomprehensible (into which it is a terrible thing to fall), that the gift is not secretly taken back again, as mostly happens. Can one dare to hope that one's own heart will

one day succeed in doing this? Do we already hope because
we have perhaps already begun to hope, and because we
think we love to some degree or desire such a love? Is it a
sufficient earnest of such audacious and yet mortally necessary
hope that one day we shall really love totally? It may seem
that the older the heart becomes the less it succeeds in doing
so. It becomes tired and dull, cold and apathetic. One
scarcely knows whether one is going on because one
cannot do anything else, stiff and numbed as one is by the
daily drill of the past, or whether one can no longer do
anything else because this inability is the blessed reward of
genuine freedom? Has virtue degenerated into routine,
momentum into futile agitation, fidelity into custom?

Where is there the fullness of time in my life, where is the
decisive hour which comprises the whole of my human
reality? It must exist. For, of course, a man does not really
put his life together piecemeal out of individual good deeds.
Each, rather, is potentially the whole, the possibility of
giving the whole life to God. If this were not so, a single
action could not decide a whole life. But this is what every
action in the full sense does—"grave" sin and also a
"grave" good deed, which must also exist and which must
be just as essentially different from a slight good deed as the
grave sin is from the venial sin. But when have I performed
important actions of that kind, which weigh as heavy as I
do, because they place a whole human being on God's
scales?

People often speak of the greatest hours, the finest and
holiest moments of human life, and mean by them—according to what is being celebrated—first communion, wedding
day, the reception of the Body of Christ, ordination and so
on. Are these events the turning-points of life which we are
seeking? Are they the fullness of eternity entering into a

moment of time? We might think so. For what could be
greater and more decisive, for example, than the moment
when man actually enjoys the bread of eternity which is the
Body of the Lord who has given himself to death for us?
And yet everyone knows that it is not only possible to
receive unworthily this bread which is the fullness of time
and so eat life to one's condemnation; everyone also knows
that with the fullness of the sacrament one does not always
receive the fullness of what that sacrament signifies and of
itself contains, the fullness of grace. This is so even if it is
not received unworthily. Not every reception of the fullness
of time is a reception of the fullness of my time. One can live
in the moment of Christ and yet one's own life may pass
dead and empty, or at least very unfulfilled, through its own
time. It would indeed be wonderful if in such sacramental
form the fullness of one's own time were found, if the
fullness of time were present here and now in my life. Then
everything would be there. The eternal plenitude of God
would be present, and this inner presence would be tangibly
present in its own manifestation, which could not be plainer,
at once personal and ecclesial, vitally concrete and liturgical.
The plenitude would be present fulfilled in the sign, in the
symbol of the banquet of eternity, of the banquet of perfect
accomplishment. One would empty the chalice of one's own
life completely and it would be perceptibly one with the
chalice of Christ. It can be so, and so it perhaps ought to be.
But we cannot in fact say whether God has intended for
everyone that the decisive hour of his life is to occur precisely when the sacramental sign of the fulfilment of the world
and of the individual is set up, in blessing and forgiveness,
in the individual's life. It may be, after all, that only a small
part of this grace is received, and only a part of the
grace for which there would in fact be room in the

heart, if it were not more cowardly and niggardly than it need be.

It is therefore possible that the greater hour, the time of greater plenitude, may occur where the sign (in the wider sense) is poorer and more ambiguous and not an *opus operatum*. It may be that one person will drain the chalice of his life with his life and his death in an hour which is not that of the eucharistic meal, although even so he lives this hour of his in dependence on the hour of Christ. For Christ acquired everyone's own hour in his, that hour which becomes present in the sacrifice and meal of the Mass. It is possible that someone may suddenly break through all the barriers which previously had fenced around his anxious egoism and emerge into the vastness of God, in a silent, unnoticed resignation, in an apparently small sacrifice. Perhaps he himself does not notice much about it, nothing that he would think worth entering in his diary. It is only that he has suddenly become so open. There is suddenly something nameless and mysterious present, colourless as it were and indescribable. But everything is different. This reality that is present cannot be set side by side with the other things which fill out the domain of life like a lumber-room. It cannot be compared with them and classified with them in agreement or contrast. The man has renounced, has set out, relinquished. And now he is suddenly everywhere and possesses all, thinking perhaps it is "nothing" because it is everything. He needs no ground to support him any more because he himself has become something like a poised totality, supporting himself (in God's totality) without falling because there is nothing onto which in his solitude and renunciation he could fall.

It is possible that someone may be frightened of this silent infinity which has opened out to him, not in abstract thoughts but in the experience of accepting the amplitude of his being as mind. He has fled back as if in terror to what is familiar in his life, to tangible human beings, to limited duties, to explicitly formulated precepts. And then he does not properly realize that while all these things are certainly necessary (if mind and not fanaticism is to prevail), they are not needed in order to flee from the other. They are there as the way of accomplishing genuine acceptance of the infinity which is really to be found in them and which is not merely set before us as a reward for our finite good works. In these good works, if they have the weighty character of which we have spoken, there is, of course, grace. Now this grace is, ultimately, God himself, the "uncreated grace", the eternal Spirit of love. That is the God who is himself present in those works. He is not only promised to good works, it is he in his own reality who gives these works only so that they may be what they should and must be (if they are to be something of value at all, that is, "saving acts"): gates open into the free infinity of God. Naturally moral good works and sentiments (if and where they exist purely as such) would be events which, closed in themselves, would be rewarded with something which was God's gift, but not God himself. The "good works" of the professed or anonymous Christian contain the infinity of God himself as the condition of their possibility (and this is therefore called grace) and as their reward (called eternal life). And since God has willed no other world but one into which he has given himself and not merely his created effects, it is the case that all that is finite is only meaningful as an outlet into immeasurable, silent and incomprehensible infinity.

Consequently it is possible that an onion or two thrown over the garden fence to a poor man may be a decisive turning-point—a little kindness which really forgets to look

for gratitude, forgiveness which does not notice at all that
it is forgiving, a drop of blood flowing from the heart and
falling somewhere, impossible really to say where, but
without bitterness; silent endurance of mortal pain almost
without knowing why, or whether one will be able to. Or
someone is entirely alone and does not flee from the solitude
or mirror himself in it. Or someone is decent in a quite
commonplace way and as a result is simply regarded as a
fool, yet is not up in arms about the madness of a world that
regards the just man as a fool. He does not bestow on himself (as a substitute for the praise of others) the consolation
of honour and recognition for his decency. He does not
secretly store this up, in order to bring it up again later and
collect the praise of the world, or at least of his friend or his
wife when he complains of the injury done to him. He is
simply decent, and that is that. That is the wonder of quite
unselfconscious decency, a decency that has become quite
naïve once more and which is the pure love of God in the
everyday world. Or someone does his duty; he does not
commit adultery, in deed or in thought, although this
obligation of fidelity seems like death to him, and he feels as
if he were obliterating his very self. Or someone prays.
And suddenly he has forgotten that he is praying, he has
forgotten that he wants something (and is therefore trying
to get what he wants), he has forgotten he is speaking. There
is only one there: God himself, silent, mute, but there,
nameless, inexpressible and incomprehensible, incompar-
able and unutterable, but there. He is there almost because
we are no longer there, grasped because we abandon self
and depart from ourselves. He is there because we are finally
no longer at home in ourselves, but—but it is no longer
possible to express this further; for if one tried to say it in
the very moment of leaving self behind, one would already

have turned back into the definable limits of one's own statement and one's own reality. If one states it (which one sometimes has to), one does not by making the statement perform the action which the statement is about.

Such decisive hours do in fact exist. They can exist. But one does not have them merely by talking about them. For an able man can talk about them because he has heard about them from others or because he has detected the inevitable remnant of them which as the mark of spirit and grace is found even in the most unspiritual and graceless deeds and experiences of man. For we would cease to be spirit (which we are even if we are whetting the knife to kill like wild beasts), we would cease to be constantly "tempted" by grace (which we always are), if we had experienced nothing at all of what is actually accomplished only in such decisive hours. But not every experience is an experience accepted and grasped with the utmost strength of the heart. We have not the fullness of time and eternity contained in our heart simply because we have enjoyed a slight taste of it and are philosophizing grandly about this small sample.

And so the question remains: has such a decisive hour of the fullness of my time occurred? A foolish question. One cannot really ask it in that way. For, of course, it would be of no use to me if I could make such a statement about an earlier moment of my life. Perhaps I can make it. Perhaps I can conjecture that it was when as a child at my first communion I invited the Lord to come into the young heart that loved him. But if I raise the question, I am obviously asking because I think that what happened then matters to me now. And that is in fact false. For all that matters is the fullness of my time which has not elapsed. It really only matters to me if now or tomorrow such an hour of eternity occurs. For as long as one is a pilgrim, as long as time is still

time, each moment is like a relay runner with a torch, who
has not only to keep the burning light for himself but has
also to hand it on to the next man. Only when the latter
grasps it and carries it on has the former's run any value
and validity. Life is not really composed of parts, when it is
spirit and not physics that is in question; but the whole runs
as an indivisible unity through time, in a process of becoming through everything. I therefore have nothing simply
because I acquired it earlier, but I have what I became
earlier because in this enduring process I become it anew.
The earlier is always only the summons to bring about what
has already been, and the promise that what has already
succeeded will also succeed now. It is therefore only out of
very incidental theoretical curiosity or in the sorrow of
contrition aiming at transforming past into future that one
can turn back to one's past, in order to seek out what lofty
hours of eternity occurred in it.

Instead of asking, therefore, whether such a decisive hour
has already occurred in our life, poor and empty as it is, full
of illusion even in the so-called good which we have done,
it would be better to ask where is such an hour coming from
to me out of what is still to come? I have to find it in what is
coming towards me. And that is also where I must seek the
past hours. For only if they are there will the hours which
God in his grace may have bestowed on me in the past
remain for me. The treasure of the past is the freedom of
the future. For we have, of course, acted in order to be able
to act, loved in order to begin to learn love. Out of the future
with God's grace which is without repentance, there really
comes to me once again my whole past, for it to be preserved
or redeemed. For what can be lost by someone who finds
God, and what opportunity is missed if we still have the
good fortune of having a heart and the ability to love God

with our whole heart? God's just anger, however, falls on those who do not believe with their whole heart the blessed message of that grace of his which is without repentance, which is our whole opportunity for life. The kind of realism which simply knows what is in oneself and in man generally forgets what is realest of all, God, the eternal future and man's glorious grace of making such a future his own. The fulfilment of this total possibility need not always and everywhere take place to the accompaniment of emotion and tears of joy as we should no doubt like it to do. It is to the tired and worn heart, burnt to dry ash by the invisible flame of suffering and disappointment, that this blessed opportunity has been chiefly, not least, promised: blessed are those who mourn, blessed those who thirst.

And so the new year is coming. A year like all the rest. A year of trouble and disappointment with myself and others. When God is building the house of our eternity, he puts up fine scaffolding in order to carry out the work. So fine, that we should prefer to live in it. The only fault we have to find with it is that it is taken down again. Then we call this dismantling the painful fragility of our life. We lament and become melancholy if in the prospect of a new year we think we can see nothing but the demolition of the house of our life, which in reality is being quietly built up for eternity behind this scaffolding that is put up and taken down again. No, the coming year is not a year of disappointments or a year of pleasing illusions. It is God's year. The year in which decisive hours are approaching me quietly and unobtrusively, and the fullness of my time is coming to enter my life. Shall I notice those hours? Or will they remain empty? Because to me they will seem too small, too humble and commonplace? Outwardly, of course, they will not look any different from anyone's everyday moments of good works and proper omissions. Consequently I may overlook them—the slight patience which makes life slightly more tolerable for those around me; the omission of an excuse; taking the risk of building on the good faith of someone whom I would be inclined to mistrust because I think I have had unfortunate experiences with them before; genuine acceptance of there being good grounds for someone else's criticism of me (how hard this is when something is at stake which involves my self-esteem); to allow an injury done to me to die away in myself, without prolonging it by complaints, rancour, bitterness and revenge; fidelity in prayer which is not rewarded with "consolations" or "religious experience"; the attempt to love those who get on my nerves (through their fault, of course), and not merely to put up with them by swallowing one's rage out of calculated egoism; the attempt to see in someone else's "stupidity" a different kind of intelligence which is not mine but need not necessarily be stupid on that account; the tolerance which does not pay back another's intolerance in kind; the endeavour not to trade on one's virtues as a charter for one's faults; a prompt will to improve oneself when we see sins in others and would dearly like to reform them; the firm conviction, firmly maintained against oneself, that we very willingly and very easily delude ourselves and leave a number of faults and pettinesses undisclosed which would strike us as patently obvious in anyone else; the suppressed complaint and the self-praise omitted and many other things which would only be really good if one practised them constantly, though it is true that it is better to do something than not to do anything at all, for one cannot manage everything at once.

We only need seriously to try to do such commonplace everyday things. Then they become terrible. They are almost deadly if they are not taken in careful homeopathic doses. For in all these cases we are the one who gets the worse of the deal; one has the impression of paying out more than one gets back. It brings in no returns, neither in the world, nor by a good conscience or inner recognition for so much self-made virtue; for even that loses its attraction. And then in all these trifles that go with a decent attitude (which fundamentally is very Christian, at least without realizing it), the point comes where morality actually becomes really moral and religious, the point where it becomes the gate to the infinite and eternal. Where one is rewarded by nothing more, that is, by nothing specific, whether outside or within, then in truth God is present as that "nothing", and finite loss is infinite gain. And appreciation of the latter is exercised by that loss. One pays for it in life with oneself. God is not to be had for less. We ought to learn this mysticism of everyday life. Only then does fulfilment of the law out of respect for the prescriptions of the supreme government of the universe (which can never be fully achieved and which simply irritates and makes one resentful like an overworked labourer) become voluntary striving in the spirit of the children of God. Such mysticism of everyday life is grace. Wholly and entirely grace. But that of course does not mean that there is nothing to do but impiously to wait until God's grace compels one against one's will. It "compels" in fact by bestowing the good will, and the goodwill thus given by God, viewed from below, is the great and honest endeavour of the human being himself. And this has to be carried out properly, by learning to form a taste for eternity in time by practice in the mysticism of daily life.

If this is practised, people will be found ready to see the more sublime possibilities of life, the hours of heroic sacrifices (if they are offered to them), the mortal trials, holy extravagance and follies and finally that death in which we die our own death, which is then a death in the death of Christ. How can we be equipped if we have not previously been on the watch for and, as far as possible, trained ourselves for such sublime hours, which no one can give himself, but which arrive by their own inscrutable law? Anyone who has not discovered the taste of eternity in time flees in alarm from such hours, he is afraid, feels himself overtaxed. It does not even occur to him that the great grace of life is in fact confronting him. He takes it for granted that "this" cannot be expected of him. And certainly it cannot be expected of his inner lack of courage which is the ground of his own judgment of himself.

The mysticism of everyday life should be practised. It is the contrary of that "fidelity to duty" of the pedant who, hardened in "virtue", would prefer best of all to continue for ever the existence of a minor official of the good God, provided he always received his salary punctually here below (calm and order and the "victory" of "right-thinking people" on earth). It is certain that everyday routine exists and we cannot escape most of it. Even the saints yawn sometimes, and have to shave. It is not so sure that hours will be given us which even from our point of view will be great and important. There must therefore be an eternity in everyday life. For we know that every human being we see, walking about to all appearance appallingly commonplace, is valuable enough to become an eternity, and to do this here on earth where all he seems to do is to earn a living none too easily, marry, and abuse the politicians if he is not actually watching a football match or treating us to his opinion of Picasso.

Perhaps for this very reason the decisive hours only come to us in the garb of everyday life. Many everyday situations will not be decisive turning-points at all. One cannot of course put forward one's full powers at simply every moment. And for the greatest freedom, most has to be given, because the innermost reality is founded on the profoundest capacity and this is a gift bestowed on us. To be able to put forward one's full powers in complete freedom is the greatest gift. It is not bestowed on us at every moment. Yet precisely this can be given to us in a trivial everyday situation. Who can say when this hour comes? We always act into an incalculable future, with the risk and opportunity that the incalculable implies. Suddenly, where we only faintly perceived it as we accepted the incalculable, the high fulfilment is given us. And yet it is ours because we have accepted it (though unknown) in faith.

The year of such possibilities is coming. We ought to celebrate New Year with more faith than we do, listless, fainthearted and unbelieving as we are. The future is coming. Foolish people think it comes seeking the past like a morbid and deadly obsession. In reality it comes because it wills to become eternity. The future does not become smaller but only really attains its identity when it becomes the past, the past which, in the human being who possesses God, is limitless present. The future which abides is coming. In the fullness of my time, through the decisive hours of believing, hoping and loving freedom. What will the new year bring to me? God in the fullness of my time. Who knows, perhaps even in such a way that the last passing moment will hand on the torch of eternal light to no further next moment, but that torch will itself shine forth as the eternal light. Who knows? I run, the apostle says. I do not look back. I do not think I have already laid hold, but I run in order that I may lay hold. One can also address a Maranatha to the new year. For the Lord is coming. In the new

year of my life too. What is the new year bringing me?
Jesus Christ the crucified and risen, the mystery of his death
and life in my life and death, his clear light in the toil of my
faith, his promise in the labour of my hope, his love for me
in the ever new attempt to find him by love through sharing
his lot. The year of the Lord is coming.

Beginning of Glory

If someone had already lit the fuse for a tremendous explosion, but was still waiting for the explosion which will follow with dreadful certainty, they certainly would not say that the lighting of the fuse was an event of the past. The beginning of an event which is still in course of development but is moving inexorably and irresistibly towards its culmination, is not past but is a kind of present, and already contains its future; it is a movement which continues by comprising past and present in a present real unity. These concepts must be clear if we are to attempt to say something meaningful about the Lord's resurrection.

Easter is not the celebration of a past event. The alleluia is not for what was; Easter proclaims a beginning which has already decided the remotest future. The resurrection means that the beginning of glory has already started. And what began in that way is in process of fulfilment. Does it take long? It lasts thousands of years because at least that short space of time is needed for an incalculable plenitude of reality and history to force itself through the brief death-agony of a gigantic transformation (which we call natural history and world history) to its glorious fulfilment. Everything is in movement. Nothing has an abiding place here.

We are gradually finding out, at least in outline, that nature has its own orientated history, that nature is in movement, that it develops and unfolds in time and by an incomprehensible self-transcendence behind which there stands the creative power of God, attains ever higher levels of reality. We are gradually realizing that human history has its purposeful course and is not merely the eternal return of the identical ("there is nothing new under the sun"), that the nations are summoned in a certain sequence and have each their definite historical mission; that history in its totality has its pattern and an irreversible direction.

But what is the goal of this whole movement in nature, history and spirit? Is everything advancing towards a collapse, to meaninglessness and nothingness? Are we only going to lose our way? Is what happens ultimately only the demonstration of the emptiness and hollowness of all things, which are unmasked in the course of the history of nature and the world? Are all the comedies and tragedies of this history mere play-acting which can only deludedly be taken seriously while they are still going on and are not yet played out?

How far has this history already advanced? Has its meaning already emerged in this game of limitless scope? Has the ultimate, all-decisive keyword already been spoken which gave all that came earlier its meaning, and already clearly contains the outcome of the whole drama?

We Christians say that this whole history of nature and mankind has a meaning, a blessed and transfigured, all-embracing meaning, no longer mixed with meaninglessness and darkness, a meaning which is infinite reality and unity comprising all possibilities and glory in one. And when we invoke the absolute meaning in this way, we call it God. God as he is in himself is the goal of all history. He himself is at hand. All the streams of change in us flow towards him; they are not lost in the bottomless void of nothingness and meaninglessness. But when we say this, when we declare infinity to be the meaning of the finite, eternity the meaning of time and God himself (by grace) to be the purport of his creature, we are not speaking simply of a distant, not yet wholly realized ideal, which we hope vaguely may be realized one day but which for the moment and for an incalculable time is still a distant future existing only in thought.

No, we say Easter, resurrection. That means, it has already begun, the definitive future has already started. The transfiguration of the world is no ideal, no postulate, but a reality. The history of nature with all its developments and self-transcendence has already—though for the moment only in its first exemplar—reached its unsurpassable culmination: material reality which, wholly transfigured, is for eternity the glorious Body of God. The most tremendous and definitive self-transcendence of the material world (through the grace-given power of God alone of course) has already taken place. It has leapt beyond itself into the infinity of God's spirituality and, in this upward flight into God's immeasurable flame, it has not been consumed but has survived, definitively transfigured.

If we thought about it correctly, we Christians would really have to say that we, not the others, are the most radical materialists, for we say that God's pure and substantial self-utterance (the divine Word of God) has a true body for all eternity. The history of humanity, so we say when we celebrate Easter, has already reached its goal in a representative or, rather, in *the* representative of this whole history (in him and through him for the others). And this has happened where not simply spirit and glorified soul, but the one human being in his totality who acted and suffered this history of his, attained perfect fulfilment, where everything abides, nothing is lost and everything is disclosed as meaningful and glorious. This end which is the beginning of the fulfilment of all things, has arrived and has manifested itself to humanity still advancing through history just as the front of a procession which has reached the goal calls back with cries of triumph to those still marching: We are there, we have found the goal and it is what we hoped it would be.

The place at which such a beginning of the end and completion has appeared is called Jesus of Nazareth, crucified and risen. Because his tomb is empty, because he who was dead has shown himself to be living in the unity of his whole concrete humanity, we know that everything has already really begun to be well. Almost everything is still on the way. But on the way to a goal which is not a utopian ideal but an already existent reality.

Man likes to give half answers. He likes to escape to where he does not have to make a clear decision. That is understandable. We are travellers and consequently in a condition in which everything, meaning and meaninglessness, death and life, is still mixed together, half finished, incomplete. But it cannot remain so. It is moving on. And the end cannot be other than clear and plain. Consequently reality compels us, whether we wish or not, to give a plain answer in our own lives. And so the question is put to us: Death or life? Meaning or meaninglessness? Ideals which are nebulously inconclusive or real facts? If by faith and action we plainly decide for meaning and life as facts, and consider life and death as mere *ideals* to be inadequate, if we affirm life and meaning as a fact, not half-heartedly but whole-heartedly in endless magnitude and scope, then whether we know it or not we have said Easter. And we Christians know this. We know that the reality of Easter is not simply the essence hidden in the depth of our life but is the truth and reality of our faith called by its name and explicitly professed. And so we comprise the whole history of nature and of mankind in a celebration which in rite contains the actual reality celebrated, and we make the ultimate statement about it: I believe in the resurrection of the body (flesh) and life everlasting. I believe that the beginning of the glory of all things has already come upon us, that we, apparently so lost, wandering and seeking far away, are already encompassed by infinite blessedness. For the end has already begun. And it is glory.

A Faith that Loves the Earth

It is difficult in well-worn human words to do justice to the joy of Easter. Not simply because all the mysteries of the Gospel have difficulty in penetrating the narrow limits of our being and because it is even more difficult for our language to contain them. The message of Easter is the most human news brought by Christianity. That is why we have most difficulty in understanding it. It is most difficult to be, do and believe what is truest, closest and easiest. For we men of today live by the tacitly assumed and therefore to us all the more self-evident prejudice that what is religious is purely a matter of the innermost heart and the highest point of the mind, something which we have to do for ourselves alone and which therefore has the difficulty and unreality of the thoughts and moods of the heart. But Easter says that God has done something. God himself. And his action has not merely lightly touched the heart of some human being here and there, so that it trembles at the inexpressible and nameless. God has raised his Son from the dead. God has called the flesh to life. He has conquered death. He has done something and triumphed where it is not at all a question merely of interior sensibility but where, despite all our praise of the mind, we are most really ourselves, in the reality of the earth, far from all that is purely thought and feeling, where we learn what we are—mortal children of the earth.

We are children of this earth. Birth and death, body and earth, bread and wine—such is our life. The earth is our home. Certainly, for all this to be so and to be splendid, mind has to be mingled with it like a secret essence, the delicate, sensitive, perceptive mind which gazes into the infinite, and the soul which makes everything living and light. But mind and soul have to be *there*, where we are, on the earth and in the body. They have to be there as the eternal radiance of earthly things, not like a pilgrim who, not understood and himself an alien, wanders once like a ghost across the world's stage in a brief episode. We are too much the children of this earth to want to emigrate from it for ever one day. And even if heaven has to bestow itself for earth to be endurable, it has itself to come down and stand over this abiding earth as a light of blessedness and itself break forth as radiance from the dark bosom of the earth.

We belong here. We cannot become unfaithful to the earth, not out of autocratic self-will, which would not suit the sons of serious, humble mother-earth, but because we must be what we are. But we suffer from a secret and mortal sorrow which lodges in the very centre of our earthly nature. The earth, our great mother, is itself in distress. It groans under its transitoriness. Its most joyful festivities suddenly resemble the beginning of funeral rites and when we hear its laughter we tremble in case in a moment tears will be mingled with it. The earth bears children who die, who are too weak to live for ever and who have too much mind to be able entirely to renounce eternal joy. Unlike the beasts of the earth, they see the end before it is there and they are not compassionately spared conscious ex-

perience of that end. The earth bears children whose
hearts know no limits, and what the earth gives them is
too beautiful for them to despise and too poor to enrich
them, the insatiable. And because the earth is the scene
of this unhappy discord between the great promise which
haunts them and the meagre gift which does not satisfy
them, the earth becomes a fertile source of its children's
guilt, for they try to tear more from the earth than it
can rightly give. It can complain that it itself became so
inharmonious through the primordial sin of the first man
on earth, whom we call Adam. But that does not alter the
fact that the earth is now an unhappy mother, too living
and too beautiful to be able to send its children away even
to conquer a new home of eternal life in another world, and
too poor to give them as fulfilment what it has contributed
to give them as longing. And because the earth is always
both life and death, it mostly brings neither, and the sad
mixture of life and death, exultation and lament, creative
action and monotonous servitude is what we call our
everyday life. And so we are here on the earth, our home,
and yet it is not enough. The adventure of emigrating from
what is earthly won't do, not out of cowardice but out of a
fidelity imposed on us by our own nature.

What are we to do? Listen to the message of the resurrection of the Lord. Has Christ the Lord risen from the dead
or not? We believe in his resurrection and so we confess:
he died, descended into the realm of the dead and rose again
the third day. But what does that mean, and why is it a
blessing for the children of the earth?

The Son of the Father has died, he who is the Son of man.
He who is at once the eternal plenitude of the godhead, self-
sufficient, limitless and blessed as Word of the Father before
all ages *and* the child of this earth as son of his blessed

mother. He who is both the Son of God's plenitude and the child of earth's need, has died. But the fact that he died does not mean (as in a really un-Christian way we "spirituals" short-sightedly think) that his spirit and soul, the vessel of his eternal godhead have freed themselves from the world and the earth, and as it were fled into the immensity of God's glory beyond the world because the body which bound them to the earth was shattered in death and because the murderous earth showed that the child of eternal light could find no home in its darkness. We say "died" and immediately add "descended into the realm of the dead and rose again". And this gives the "died" quite a different sense from the world-forsaking sense which we are tempted to attribute to death. Jesus himself said that he would descend into the heart of the earth (Mt 12:40), that is, into the heart of all earthly things where everything is linked into one and where in the midst of that unity death and futility sit. In death he descended there. By a holy ruse of eternal life he allowed himself to be overcome by death, allowed death to swallow him into the innermost centre of the world so that, having descended to the primordial forces and the radical unity of the world, he might establish his divine life in it for ever. Because he died, he belongs in very truth to this earth. For although the man—the soul, as we say—enters in death into direct relation to God, it is only when the body of a man is laid in the earth that he enters into definitive unity with that mysterious single basis in which all spatio-temporal things are linked and in which they have as it were the root of their life. The Lord descended into death into this lowest and deepest of all the visible creation. He is there now, and not futility and death. In death he became the heart of the earthly world, divine heart in the very heart and centre of the world where this, prior even to its unfolding in space and time, sinks its roots into God's omnipotence. It was from this one heart of all earthly things in which fulfilled unity and nothingness could no longer be distinguished and from which their whole destiny derived, that he rose. And he did not rise in order finally to depart from hence, not so that the travail of death which gave birth to him anew might transfer him to the life and light of God and he would leave behind him the dark bosom of the earth empty and without hope. For he rose again in his *body*. That means he has already begun to transform this world into himself. He has accepted the world for ever. He has been born again as a child of the earth, but of the transfigured, liberated earth, the earth which in him is eternally confirmed and eternally redeemed from death and futility. He rose, not to show that he was leaving the tomb of the earth once and for all, but in order to demonstrate that precisely that tomb of the dead—the body and the earth—has finally changed into the glorious, immeasurable house of the living God and of the God-filled soul of the Son. He did not go forth from the dwelling-place of earth by rising from the dead. For he still possesses, of course, definitively and transfigured, his body, which is a piece of the earth, a piece which still belongs to it as a part of its reality and its destiny. He rose again to reveal that through his death the life of freedom and beatitude remains established for ever within the narrow limits and sorrow of the earth, in the depth of its heart.

What we call his resurrection and unthinkingly regard as his own personal destiny, is simply, on the surface of reality as a whole, the first symptom in experience of the fact that behind so-called experience (which we take so seriously) everything has already become different in the true and decisive depth of all things. His resurrection is like the first eruption of a volcano which shows that in the interior of the world God's fire is already burning, and this will bring everything to blessed ardour in his light. He has risen to show that that has already begun. Already from the heart of the world into which he descended in death, the new forces of a transfigured earth are at work. Already in the innermost centre of all reality, futility, sin and death are vanquished and all that is needed is the short space of time which we call history *post Christum natum*, until everywhere and not only in the body of Jesus what has really already begun will be manifest. Because he did not begin to save and transfigure the world with the superficial symptoms but started with its innermost root, we creatures of the surface think that nothing has happened. Because the waters of suffering and guilt are still flowing where *we* are standing, we think the deep sources from which they spring have not yet dried up. Because wickedness is still inscribing its runes on the face of the earth, we conclude that in the deepest heart of reality love is extinct. But all that is merely appearance, the appearance which we take to be the reality of life.

He has risen because in death he conquered and redeemed for ever the innermost centre of all earthly reality. And having risen, he has held fast to it. And so he has remained. When we confess him as having ascended to God's heaven, that is only another expression for the fact that he withdraws from us for a while the tangible manifestation of his glorified humanity and above all that there is no longer any abyss between God and the world. Christ is already in the midst of all the poor things of this earth, which we cannot leave because it is our mother. He is in the wordless expectation of all creatures which without knowing it, wait to share in the glorification of his body. He is in the history of the earth, the blind course of which in all victories and all breakdowns is moving with uncanny precision towards his day, the day on which his glory, transforming all things, will break forth from its own depths. He is in all tears and in all death as hidden rejoicing and as the life which triumphs by appearing to die. He is in the beggar to whom we give, as the secret wealth which accrues to the donor. He is in the pitiful defeats of his servants, as the victory which is God's alone. He is in our powerlessness as the power which can allow itself to seem weak, because it is unconquerable. He is even in the midst of sin as the mercy of eternal love patient and willing to the end. He is there as the most secret law and the innermost essence of all things which still triumphs and prevails even when all order and structure seems to be disintegrating. He is with us like the light of day and the air which we do not notice, like the hidden law of a movement which we do not grasp, because the part which we ourselves experience is too short for us to discern the formula of the movement. But he is there, the heart of this earthly world and the secret seal of its eternal validity.

Consequently we children of this earth may love it, must love it. Even where it is fearful and afflicts us with its distress and mortal destiny. For since he has entered into it for ever by his death and resurrection, its misery is merely temporary and simply a test of our faith in its innermost mystery, which is the risen Christ. That this is the secret meaning of its distress is not our experience. Indeed it is not. It is our faith. The blessed faith which defies all experience. The faith which can love the earth because it is the "body" of the risen Christ or is becoming it. We therefore do not need to leave it. For God's life dwells in it. If we seek the God of infinity (and how could we fail to?) *and* the familiar earth as it is and as it is to become, in order to be our eternal home in freedom, then one way leads to both. For in the Lord's resurrection God has shown that he has taken the earth to himself for

ever. *Caro cardo salutis*, said one of the ancient Fathers of the
Church with an untranslatable play on words: the flesh is
the hinge of salvation. The reality beyond all the distress of
sin and death is not up yonder; it has come down and dwells
in the innermost reality of our flesh. The sublimest religious
sentiment of flight from the world would not bring the God
of our life and of the salvation of this earth down from the
remoteness of his eternity and would not reach him in that
other world of his. But he has come to us himself. He has
transformed what we are and what despite everything we
still tend to regard as the gloomy earthly residue of our
spiritual nature: the flesh. Since then mother earth has only
borne children who are transformed. For his resurrection
is the beginning of the resurrection of all flesh.

One thing is needed, it is true, for his action, which we can
never undo, to become the benediction of our human reality.
He must break open the tomb of our hearts. He must rise
from the centre of our being also, where he is present as
power and as promise. There he is still in movement. There
it is still Holy Saturday until the last day which will be the
universal Easter of the cosmos. And that resurrection takes
place under the freedom of our faith. Even so it is *his* deed.
But an action of his which takes place as our own, as an
action of loving belief which takes us up into the tremendous movement of all earthly reality towards its own glory,
which has begun in Christ's resurrection.

CORPUS CHRISTI

Feast of the Daily Bread

Corpus Christi is a strange feast. It celebrates what is celebrated every day in the unassuming silence of our churches:
the mystery of the altar. It displays in festive procession
what is not only shown every day but received, the holy
bread of eternal life. It lifts up outwardly what is received
elsewhere, the heavenly manna. It is almost as if the feast
were attempting specially to celebrate what in fact happens
every day, and yet fails to do so because ordinary life can
celebrate more fittingly than the high festival what is
ultimately in question: the fact that we receive this bread of
eternal life as pilgrims between time and eternity, each day
anew until the journey is at an end and God unveiled becomes for us the eternal bread of glory. Whether this is so or
not, we celebrate this feast in order that the everyday round
may not allow us to forget too much what we celebrate each
day: the meal of those who are pilgrims to eternal life.

How exactly this meal suits our needs! We are still
travelling as pilgrims, never settled, always moving on, in
the provisional. Consequently we walk among shadows and
symbols in the darkness of faith. That is an unavoidable lot
and its pain is salutary and should not surprise us. The
highest is, after all, furthest away and remains a prize prom-

ised only to voluntary fidelity in what is provisional. Yet we should like to have this highest at once even now although, or rather precisely because, we are wandering in search of it. For how could we go on pilgrimage if we were not already aware of the powers of eternity in us? How could we hope, if what we hope for were *only* far away? One can only seek God with God, and we should not seek if we had not yet already found, if he himself did not permit himself to be found by us day by day. And so the promise and the possession must both be true: way and goal are simultaneously present, God is with us, hidden under the veil of his own creatures. If therefore the holy banquet of eternity is prepared for us here in time, it is in a way which the sober humility of pilgrims such as we may expect: simple and ordinary, hidden under the signs of commonplace, everyday earthly life, under which the real meaning has to be believed and firmly held in hope and love. And so the Lord has prepared this meal: for the senses a sign, in appearance a little bread and wine, such as usually nourish our bodies and cheer our minds. But when at his command, by his power and with his words *the* commemoration of his last meal is celebrated, and this latter is truly brought into our own present moment, then the inner truth and reality of these signs is himself in his flesh and blood. He becomes the bread of limitless strength and the wine of inexpressible joy. He himself makes his body a sign for us in our time of what he wishes to be for us in his Spirit: God giving his own life to his poor creature. He becomes for us now as we receive the bread of the altars, what he is in himself: the earthly reality by which God's eternity has entered into the narrow limits of our finitude. A man's head bends over what looks like an ordinary piece of bread—over what in fact merely looks like a semblance of real bread—his hand reaches for a cup such as usually contains merely the drink of this earthly life, and then there happens what is the innermost goal of *everything* that happens. God and the believing heart each from their own side break through all the sinister walls which at other times so infinitely separate them. They meet in him who is both, in whom such a unity already occurred definitively and corporeally, in the Lord, who in one person is the eternal Word from on high and the son of the earth from the Virgin's womb. We hold the body of this earth which was born and was sacrificed in pain; we penetrate once more into the depth of what he suffered long ago, when we hold what he took from us. And we are abidingly where we and he have remained, in the centre with God. Sacred banquet in which Christ is received, the memory of his Passion is renewed, the soul is filled with grace and the earnest of future glory is bestowed.

Yet we commonplace people make this mystery of eternal life in this dying time so commonplace! Look how the priest performs his sublime office—morosely, impelled by objective duty, as though he were carrying out some duty of this world and not the liturgy in which the light and blessedness of heaven are contained. Consider the narrow and barren hearts into which the Lord descends and which at best do not know what to say to him except the few selfish desires which make up their everyday round. Alas, we Christians. In this sacrament we receive both the pure blessedness of heaven and the refined transfigured essence of the bitter-sweet fruit of this earth. We receive it, to be sure, as though wrapped in the hard shell of custom but nevertheless in all truth. And we receive it as though nothing were happening. Weary and lazy we take the same heart back home from the table of God into the narrow rooms of our lives where we are more at home than in

God's upper room. We offer the Son in sacrifice and want to refuse our hearts. We play the divine game of the liturgy and we are not in earnest about it. We have perhaps a good will but it has so little power over the dull heaviness of our heart. But perhaps even this belongs to the sign, when God is already hastening towards his creature even here in time, and when even now the banquet of eternal life is celebrated in advance. If the supper of eternal life is prepared in the narrow houses of time, it is not surprising that the needy come to it, and that their small minds and meagre hearts do not yet realize at all what is to be theirs. It is understandable that we are rather disturbed and feel our strength overtaxed and, as it were, almost driven to irritated reserve by such lavishness on God's part. For it is after all still grace, his blessed grace, if we come at all, if we do after all have supper at his table, if we only come, if we only drag ourselves to him, we who are dreary, bent, weary and burdened. He welcomes us even if he does not find in our eyes radiant joy at his presence. For he has of course descended into all the abysses of this earth; it does not offend him to have to enter the dull narrowness of our hearts, or if only a small spark of love and good will glimmer there. In the patience which God has with us weaklings, the highest sacrament is meant to be the sacrament of our every day.

But because that is so, because we only come from so far away, because we make the feast a burden and an effort because it is a daily one, it is right for us at least once in the year to celebrate a feast of those feasts which we celebrate every day. A feast to celebrate the fact that what is usual is most unusual, what is done every day is the substance of eternity, the bread of earth God's coming among us and the beginning of the transfiguration of all earthly reality. Let us therefore celebrate today in mourning but with consolation the fact that every day we so unfestively celebrate the mystery of the Lord, a feast of joy that despite this he is with us all days until the end. Let us keep a feast of the past which is present in the commemoration of the supper and death of the Lord which truly annuls all distance of time, a feast of the future which under the veil of the sacrament already even now has what all the future is to bring, the presence of the God of eternal love. Every day God prepares his feast for us, the holy supper of the Lord. Today, on the feast of Corpus Christi, we ourselves ought in some way to prepare a feast for God in warm gratitude for his giving us every day that festive meal in which we pilgrims receive strength and joy so that here on the roads of time we may arrive home for the banquet of eternal life.

On the Way with the Lord

The Church today carries its sacrament in festive procession through all the fields of human reality. Joyfully singing hymns it walks through the streets of the world and shows to this world with an almost frightening exuberance and exultation its most intimate possession, the blessed presence of its Lord. In this solemn action, procession and singing, the Church apparently does not pay much heed to whether we ourselves feel festive and joyful, or whether we are really able sincerely to do what we are called upon to do on this feast-day. The Church is bold enough each year on a certain particular day to hold a procession of a kind which one can only really hold if one is joyful, free, inwardly unhampered by the burden of ordinary life. For that reason alone one might perhaps be disturbed. Can I join in the celebrations? Is my own heart not too heavy? In fact when we hear the rejoicing, see the solemn ceremony and at the same time consider what is being shown there, our very heart misgives us. Not that one is condemning this festive rejoicing, God forbid. Where else should men hold festival if not here, when we profess that we sinners, weak, empty and fettered, are liberated, given the freedom of the holy glory of God? What is frightening and inconceivable about these people singing and holding festival is that it is death they are celebrating with such jubilation. For it is written: As often as you do this, you proclaim the Lord's death until he comes. The Lord instituted this sacrament on the night when he was betrayed into death. He said: Do this in remembrance of me, so that we should celebrate in perpetual remembrance the sacrifice in which his body was shattered and his blood shed and he allowed his forsaken soul to fall into the hands of the incomprehensible God. It is true indeed that our very heart misgives us. For jubilantly under the blue sky in the scent of the flowers and of incense, under arcades of sacred song, we bear the sign of a man's death, and not just any man's, but the death of him who was the Word of God made flesh. How incomprehensible is man and his existence that such a thing can be, that the uttermost darkness of fall into the lowest bottomless pit can become a festival of childlike, innocent joy. We are proclaiming the death of the Lord until he comes again. Do not let us forget that today. Remembrance of that death is not death to joy, but its unfathomable root, from which the true joy of this day indescribably flows as though from an inexhaustible spring.

Look at these people walking in procession! In festive clothes, they are singing and moving forward almost as David once did when he danced before the ark of the covenant. Where are they going? If one has the courage to ask and the courage to answer the question seriously and in all its aspects, completely and without illusions, can one avoid one answer, even if it is only a part of the complete answer: they are going forward to death? For the place of their procession is, of course, time which never stands still. And where time is, death sits, the end of the matter, even of the movement in time. So when those who are walking have finished their festive procession, they are already inexorably a few hours nearer to death, their own death, precisely so much nearer than if they had bitterly wept during those hours. And after this solemn procession, of course, things do not cease, life goes on. For those in the procession go further, on other paths. But these paths or those, these stony ways and those wide roads are nevertheless only sections of one and the same road. And this leads to where there is no going on, where everything that moves and advances has an end, the one end.

It is strange that those who are walking in this way and on this day have decorated the outward road of their interior journey to death, bear on this serious walk through the festive streets precisely him who died just as they must die, who died for those who have to die, who died for them because they have to die. It is he they have with them on their way. They carry the one who was slain, towards their own death. Why do they do this? Are they not taking death to their hearts if they bear this dead man, whereas they are after all moving in order that the stop, the end, may not happen too quickly? Why do they hold this procession of people destined for death, with him who was slain, to the accompaniment of songs instead of tears of hopeless despair? Precisely because he died. Because it was the Son of God, who is life itself, who died. Because with them they have him who shared their lot, though he is the God whom nothing befalls. Because it is he who gave his life voluntarily, though none could take it from him, because it is he who could overcome death in death, because it is he who went down into the ultimate void in order to fill it with eternal life. Because they have him with them on the *via dolorosa* of their life, they may laugh and sing and transform part of their serious journey into a Corpus Christi procession. They can also weep. They can take part just as they are, dusty from the main roads of life, rather tired and dull, not really inclined either to laugh or cry, existing as it were half-way between the lowest depths and the blissful heights of existence, travelling like pilgrims on a road which it is impossible to identify either as *via triumphalis* or *via dolorosa*. They may and can be all these things if they go forward and he is there. For if he is there, it is as one who has wept the tears of their death for them, who has gone down into the lowest depth of death, where no mortal except him has been. While he accompanies us now in the sacrament (as he does every day in the grace of his spirit) those who walk invoke him who suffered under Pontius Pilate, died and was buried, descended into hell. But this is said of him who is the eternal Word of the Father, who is wisdom, light and strength, life and resurrection. When the sign of the ultimate and most terrible death is raised in blessing over those who are on their knees, it means that in the sign of death which blesses mortal men on their way to death, life is present, not death, the life which made of death itself the victory of life. And so, once a year for us Christians our road becomes a *via triumphalis* and we walk behind one who, bearing life in himself, became our life by sharing our death. He goes on ahead. His sacrament announces his death. And also ours. Since he goes on before us, he does not delude us with any stupefying trivialities. He says, you share my fate which you proclaim in this sacrament; you share its hardship, difficulty and inexorability. And by this solemn procession, we proclaim that his fate is ours too. And in its entirety, of which it is written, "I died and behold I am alive for evermore, and I have the keys of death and Hades" (Rev 1:18).

We cannot grasp all at once the immeasurable significance

of a procession like this with him who died and who lives. Who could comprehend God and the world, life and death, time and eternity united as they are in this festival? We can only go on walking through life, led through ever new realities, and this walk today is only a symbol of them. Sometimes the way is a pleasant one, a high road to distant destinations, another time it is a way of the Cross. Sometimes dusty field paths, in open country, but barren; sometimes forest tracks leading one knows not where. To all of them the words of scripture apply: man is not the master of his ways. But all ways ought to form one way, one of God's paths, as the psalms often say. All should link up into stretches of road leading to a goal, whether they pass through joy or death. All paths ought to lead into the free incalculability of God where there are no more paths because one has come to the end of perfect fulfilment, and this is at once trackless immensity and familiar home. If we see the sacramental path of today's procession, we shall not forget the other paths of which today's walk is only a sign, a profession of faith and a promise. During it we shall not forget the other paths, those of our own lives; the ways of those who are weary, poor and burdened and perhaps do not know what the hidden goal of this apparently erratic and aimless wandering is; the way of those who, ruled by the enemies of Christianity, are not allowed to make joyful processions—but have to follow the real way of the Cross of faith behind him who bore the Cross. We will remember and pray God to give us some day the grace that at our end a very small procession, even if it only consists of a silently praying priest in everyday clothes, will turn into the street of our life in its last moments and so become the provision for the journey, the viaticum, of eternal life for us at the place where our course goes no further. Then in the sacrament or, if it so pleases God, at least in the grace of the sacrament, the Lord will come with us at least the last stretch of our way. Then the pathway of this dying life in imitation of Christ will become the blessed road of eternal life leading into the unutterable glory of God.

Lord Jesus Christ, Son of the Father, sacrament of life, bread of pilgrims, viaticum and goal, way and home, may you be adored, loved and praised in your sacrament.

Lord, today is Whitsun. Today we are celebrating the day when you, raised above the highest heavens, sitting at the right hand of the Father, poured out on us the Spirit of the promise, so that you in your Spirit might remain with us all days until the end, and through him continue in us your life and death to the glory of the Father and to our salvation.

Lord, consider the spirits which oppress us and give us the spiritual gift of discernment. What gift would be more appropriate to Whitsun?

Give us the knowledge, enduring in everyday life, that if we seek and long for you, the spirit of serenity, peace and confidence, freedom and simple clarity is *your* Spirit, and every spirit of unrest and fear, of narrowness and of leaden depression is at most our spirit or is that of the dark abyss.

Give us your spirit of consolation. We know, Lord, that we should, must and can be true to you even in desolation, dryness, weakness of soul. Nevertheless we may also ask you for the spirit of consolation and strength, joy and confidence, of growth in faith, hope and love, of vigorous service and praise of your Father, for the spirit of calm and peace. Banish from our hearts spiritual desolation, darkness, confusion, inclination for base and earthly things, hopelessness and mistrust, tepidity, sadness and the feeling of abandonment, discord and the choking feeling of being far from you.

But if it pleases you to lead us by such ways, then leave us at least, we beseech you, in such hours and days, the holy spirit of fidelity, constancy and perseverance, so that we may go on our way in blind trust, maintain direction and remain true to the resolutions which we made when your light was shining on us and your joy filled our hearts. Yes, and give us rather, in the midst of such desolation, the spirit of courageous enterprise, of defiant "Now's the time!" in prayer, self-control and penance. Give us then absolute confidence that we are not abandoned by your grace even in those times of abandonment, the confidence that you are more than ever with us when unfelt, as the power which wills to be victorious in our weakness. Give us the spirit of true remembrance of the kindness of your loving visitations in the past and of vigilant watch for the tangible evidences of your love, in the future. At such times of desolation cause us to confess our sinfulness and wretchedness, humbly experience our weakness and acknowledge that you alone are the true source of all good and of all heavenly consolation.

When your consolation comes to us, let it be accompanied by the spirit of humility and of readiness to serve you even without consolation.

Give us always the spirit of courage and sturdy determination to recognize temptation and occasion of sin, not to argue with them, to make no compromise with them, but plainly to say No, because that is the simplest tactics in the fight. Give us the humility to ask for advice in puzzling

situations, without insincere loquacity and self-complacency
but also without the stupid pride which suggests we ought
always to try to manage by ourselves. Give us the spirit of
heavenly wisdom, so that we may recognize the real danger-
points of our character and life and watch and fight most
faithfully where we are most vulnerable.

Give us, that is, *your* Whitsun Spirit, the fruits of the
Spirit, which your apostle tells us are love, joy, peace,
patience, kindness, goodness, faithfulness, gentleness, self-
control. If we have this Spirit and its fruits, we are no longer
slaves of the Law but free children of God. Then the Spirit
will call in us: Abba, Father. Then he will intercede for us
with sighs too deep for words. Then he will be the anointing
oil, seal and pledge of eternal life, the spring of living water
which wells up in the heart and flows to eternal life, and
whispers, come, home to the Father.

Jesus, send us the Spirit. Give your Pentecost gift more
and more. Make the eye of our spirit clear and our spiritual
powers sensitive, so that we can distinguish your Spirit
from all others. Give us your Spirit, so that it may be true of
us that "If the Spirit of him who raised Jesus from the dead
dwells in you, he will give life to your mortal bodies also
through his Spirit who dwells in you". It is Pentecost, Lord.
Your servants and handmaids ask with the boldness you
commanded them to have. Let it be Pentecost in us also.
Now and for ever. Amen.

LOVE OF GOD AND THE NEIGHBOUR

The First Commandment

Matthew 23:34–40

A lot is said and written nowadays about love of one's neighbour. By pagans who have salvaged it from Christianity, for it is not an inheritance of their own. By Christians, for even if very little is practised, at least it has to be talked about. This is very right and proper. For it has to be preached and we have to be admonished, threatened, warned. There cannot be too much talk about love of the neighbour, provided of course that talk is not a mere pretext for doing nothing. But we must not forget all the same what we read in today's gospel: the *first* commandment is love of God. Love for *him* with all our heart, with all our soul and with all our mind. A "decent life" is no substitute for this love, nor is love of the neighbour, philanthropy or social justice. All these things are also necessary. But they are not love of God. And this is required of us—that great, living and heartfelt love which is so much the first and unique commandment, that we have to forget we are fulfilling a precept by it, and love not because it is commanded but simply because God is God.

This strange commandment does not demand a particular measurable performance, so that if we had achieved this we should have fulfilled our obligation. Love demands our very heart, what is innermost and ultimate in us, ourselves. But we will give anything away rather than ourselves; everything can be measured and filled except the heart. And this has to give itself to God for ever and without limit. Do we love God like that? Do we love him as someone who loves, who is near and faithful, who asks for our love by offering us his own heart and his own eternal love? Or is God for us only the name of a supreme world rule, thought of in an extremely impersonal way, which one respects, with which one may come into conflict, which one really only wishes to avoid by fulfilling the commandments? To fear God is almost easier than truly to love him. But precisely this love is an obligation laid on us, so much so that without this love all fear of God—would we at least had it!—would be of no avail to us. For damnation is ultimately only the despairing incapacity to love God.

Our heart is so inert and tired. It is worn out with every-day things. And God is so far away. So it seems to us, the spiritually blind and lame. Consequently our heart feels it cannot love. When love is preached to it, it remains dumb, unmoved, stubborn, and even "good will" seems incapable of commanding the heart to love. No, of ourselves we have not got the love which the first commandment speaks. Only he who demands it of us can give it to us. And so we will at least seek this love from him. We will pray for this love. If the first commandment is love of God, the first of prayers is to ask for this love. We must pray for this love. For God himself must pour out this love in our hearts by his Holy Spirit. He must give the life, light and strength of this love. He must himself love himself in us and through us in his Holy Spirit, for our love to be worthy of him.

Humble alarm at our lovelessness in regard to God is the God-effected beginning of our love. Prayer for love of God, a prayer which protests against our heart's secret and unavowed aversion from God, is our beginning of love of God and we can always make this by his grace, which is always offered to us. We have often recited in Church the formula by which the three theological virtues are "revived" (as the phrase goes). But it is to be hoped that we have also already prayed from the depth of our heart for the love which only God himself can give, although he has commanded it of us in that commandment which always remains the first. God hears such a prayer. For he has promised it to us in his most truthful word. For our part we should believe him rather than our own heart. If it prays for love, it loves, even if the poor heart feels little more than sorrow at still having fulfilled so little the first of all commandments.

The New, Single Precept of Love

We shall be concerned here with the unity of love of the neighbour and love of God[1]. Are they simply two things side by side, linked in some way by God's commandment, so that God is in fact loved, as he wills to be, if his commandment to love the neighbour is also respected and carried out as far as possible? Or are the two things more closely connected? It might, of course, be thought that God has commanded all kinds of things and that he regards as it were the fulfilment of these various precepts as a touchstone and concrete effect of what in the last resort is his sole will, namely, that man should love him, the eternal God, from his innermost centre, with his whole heart and strength. But fundamentally that is not so. The love of God and the neighbour form a much greater unity than they appear to have in the common view of them. We shall submit this to a little reflection.

In addition to the fundamental gravity of the theme, special importance also attaches to it, I think, from the

[1] Cf. also K. Rahner, "Über die Einheit von Nächstenliebe und Gottesliebe", *Geist und Leben* 38 (1965), pp. 168–85 or *Schriften zur Theologie* vol. VI (1965), pp. 277–98. In this essay the author gives a more rigorous theological proof of what is said here.

situation at the present time. It is a fact, and as Christians we should be deceiving ourselves if we tried to ignore it, that people today have considerable difficulties in the question of God. The world seems to have become as it were opaque and solid. The relation to God, the living, eternal God transcending the world, is no longer as easy as in times when people to some extent had the impression, perhaps ultimately without any real right, that the mysterious rule of God can be directly grasped everywhere in his world.

People today live in a secularized world. In the present context we need not consider how far this situation has a positive significance despite its danger. Nor why and to what extent and within what limits the henceforth secularized world is an element in the destiny of the Christian which was to be expected and can be regarded in a positive light as an opportunity for a genuine relation to God and for genuine Christian life. At all events, in the concrete the present situation is such (if I may briefly summarize what is in question here) that only where, and to the extent that, a man has a genuine, loving and really heartfelt relationship with his fellow-men, does he find God and can he convince other men that this reality which we call God exists. All merely theoretical talk on the subject, all worship even, everything explicitly religious would no longer appear credible to people today unless it were based on, comprised in and attested by genuine love, and that means love between human beings. People today have an almost radical need, I should say, to demythologize everything, to tear down all façades, abolish all taboos, and to ask what is left if we drop all pronouncements and demolish all ideologies. There really only remains one thing then, that we can only live if we love one another, if this love is genuine. Perhaps the

actual human being of today does not achieve this love, but
he knows he is under an obligation to do so. On the whole
he will be ready to acknowledge this obligation, this love,
even today as what is genuine, enduring, and not simply
ideological, as something which is not merely a topic for
pious or sublime speeches at meetings but as something that
is a necessity of life like business and food. If we Christians
did not know that this love which survives all demythologizing and abolition of taboos, in reality comprises the whole
of Christianity, though hidden as in a seed which has to
develop and come to blossom, I do not think that in our
present situation we should be equipped really to understand our Christianity. We could not bear witness to it even
today as the sustaining power which perpetually revives to
new life. That is the up-to-date reason why it is meaningful,
I think, to say something about the unity of love of God
and the neighbour.

This theme is already found, of course, in scripture.
There it is said that there are two commandments of which
the second, Jesus Christ says, is like the first. One commandment of love of God and the neighbour. Paul says that this
love is the bond of perfection; he is speaking of love of the
neighbour when he says that anyone who has it has fulfilled
the Law as such. And he says that this love is the genuine,
better way. At the same time he warns us that this love and
external outward help, though they belong together, are
not the same. For if I were to give away all I have to the
poor and delivered my body to be burned, but had not
charity, I should be nothing. He does not mean that some
feeling or interior disposition is everything. For that
interior disposition has to find expression in the activity of
life, in the real practice of love, otherwise it is all empty talk
and for all our feelings we should be nothing but sounding

brass and tinkling cymbal. And yet we see what very radical significance Paul attributes to the innermost nature of this love of the neighbour, when he says that it is the fulfilment of the Law, the bond of perfection.

All this, however, is far from self-evident and a matter of course. If I may so express it, though this would certainly be paradoxical and exaggerated, it almost looks as though Paul were not thinking of God at all, but were actually working out an atheistic ethics of Christianity.

How is the Law fulfilled if I have loved my neighbour? How is this love not merely a part, but the bond of perfection? How is it that on this love the whole of the Law and the prophets depends?—the Lord says this. For in that case surely the love of the neighbour would itself have to contain everything else, including precisely what is everything, what is ultimate and decisive: that God must be loved. If for the moment we leave John out of account, scripture does not actually tell us how it is that there are not merely two commandments, similar to one another, perhaps equally important and linked in some way, but that one is contained in the other. We might perhaps understand quite well that we only love God if we also love our neighbour. But with Paul it is clearly the case that if we love our neighbour we already love God.

How is that possible? John in his first letter perhaps takes us a little farther by asking how we can love the God whom we do not see if we do not love the brother whom we do see. Of course it may be said that that is a simple and obvious argument which really amounts to nothing more than: If you do not love the neighbour whom you have concretely and practically there in your life, how little you will succeed in loving the invisible God who is so remote from your immediate circle. But clearly John means even more, for in the fourth chapter of the First Letter of John we find the remarkable statement that God abides in us. And clearly this also contributes to make it possible that we already love God if we really love our neighbour with absolutely genuine personal commitment. And so this thesis—to express it in theoretical, pedagogical terms—amounts to this: love of God and love of the neighbour are mutually inclusive; when man acts with real unselfishness, commits himself absolutely, with real renunciation of his freedom in relation to the other human partner, and thus really performs what is meant by love of the neighbour, he already loves God. And this is so even if he does not explicitly know this, or tell himself it is so, even if he would not make God as such in explicit concepts a motive for love of his neighbour. The thesis means that by really loving his neighbour, man as it were falls or penetrates into the ultimate realities of created reality and, even if he does not explicitly say so, is really mysteriously concerned in this love with the God of his eternal, supernatural salvation. How is it possible to maintain such a thesis?

In the first place we may refer to scholastic theology. This speaks of three theological virtues, that is, three modes of human activity in which, supported by the Holy Spirit, by the Spirit of God in the depths of his own heart, man is concerned no longer simply with the realities of the world but directly with God. Three fundamental modes of man's ultimate orientation towards the God of eternal life himself in his own glory and independence of the world, so that we all become really and directly the partners of God himself. Faith, hope and love are the fundamental acts of man, in which he has dealings with God, the triune God of eternal life. And these three alone, as Paul says, remain.

Now theology says that by this divine fundamental

power of charity, in which faith and hope are already comprised and integrated, the neighbour also can and must be loved. If we as Christians really love our neighbour in a way conducive to salvation, we are not merely fulfilling one or other of God's commandments which we fulfil with his help. There actually takes place that ultimate, and really the only, eternal occurrence in our life, in which man truly comes directly to God himself.

When we love our neighbour in supernatural love of God, there takes place, and strictly speaking nowhere else, salvation, justification, divine life, eternity. There is no doubt in Catholic theology that there is such a divine virtue in which man finds his neighbour in the ultimate depth of his own being. And once again, it is not merely a question of the fact that because one loves God one regards the rest of his creatures with a certain goodwill and avoids transgressing the precepts of the beloved God in regard to these other human creatures. In genuine supernatural love of the neighbour, love of God is accomplished by the power of God himself.

Now it might be thought that by saying this in accordance with Catholic theology, we have already reached the point aimed at. Yet that is not quite the case. Of course, when someone loves his neighbour's very self with the consciousness of faith and from the motive of divine love of God himself it is clear from what has been said that *caritas,* the divine virtue of love of God, is accomplished. Catholic theology has been in agreement on this for centuries as a matter of course, and expounds it more or less as we have just briefly indicated. I should like, however, to try to carry the radical character of this thesis somewhat further.

I should like to say that where man really abandons himself and loves his neighbour with absolute selflessness, he has already come to the silent, inexpressible mystery of God and that such an act is already based on that divine self-communication which we call grace and which gives the act of which it is the ground its saving meaning and importance for eternity.

We may raise the question from quite a different angle. We meet many people who are not professedly Christians and do not even wish to be. Let us assume that such a person were really to love with ultimate radical selflessness his neighbour, the brother whom he sees. Then what has actually happened? Only a very good deed worthy of recognition but to which ultimately the most important thing is lacking? Or is there already present there an ultimate relation to God which ought indeed to develop and as it were receive its name, which still has to be measured and named in its ultimate, inexpressible but real dimensions in relation to God, but which is nevertheless already there? This is precisely what I mean when I say that the love of God, charity, is always and everywhere present in that ultimate, genuine, radical love of the neighbour in which a man really engages himself and the ultimate strength of his being and gives himself. Not, of course, because the natural structure of such an act necessarily entails this, but because we live under the universal saving will of God. We live in a world which always and everywhere is directed by the secret grace of God towards the eternal life of God, always and everywhere where a man does not expressly shut himself off by really culpable unbelief from this innermost supernatural, grace-given dynamism of the world.

Now an act of love of the neighbour is not simply one moral action among others, but basically it is the fundamental act of human moral reality, of man himself. Cognition is immanent presence to self, and freedom is ultimately free, personal, deliberately final and definitive disposition over oneself.

Both of these, however, can only take place in loving communication with a personal partner. For man, as a spiritual, personal subject, the world is primarily the human world around him. We do not simply live in an environment in which every imaginable kind of thing exists. That world has an inner structure deriving from the human subject and from the reality which man encounters. Ultimately it is a communication by love with another human person. The whole world of things with which we have to deal, even in economic life, society etc., is fundamentally only the material, the condition and the consequence of loving communication with other persons. Man disposes over himself in radical freedom productive of eternal consequences, and this self-disposal in the last resort is simply either the loving openness in regard to the human partner or a final self-closing in egoism, which throws man into the damning, deadly isolation of the lost. This fundamental act is of course only possible because man is dynamically oriented towards the absolute of reality, that is, because in fact in a non-explicit, unanalysed way he has to do with God. For we do not begin to have something to do with God only when we explicitly invoke him, or when we expressly name and profess this mystery towards which we are always moving and which alone bestows the possibility of spiritual freedom and love. Always and everywhere in the activity of cognition and most certainly in that of love, we have to do with God in an implicit way. And if a human being in the fundamental act which actualizes his human reality, adopts an attitude of love towards his fellow-men, then this fundamental act of his life, through the universal divinizing saving will of God which is everywhere at work even outside the Church, is supported by God's Holy Spirit and his grace and at least implicitly and tacitly but really, is at the same time an act of charity, of the love of God.

In a more precise description of what love of the neighbour means, we should of course have to show how in reality it always approaches the mystery of God even if it does not expressly wish or intend to. If we are silent, if we forgive, if without reward we give ourselves wholeheartedly and are detached from ourselves, we are reaching out into a limitlessness which exceeds any assignable bounds and which is nameless. We are reaching out towards the holy mystery which pervades and is the ground of our life. We are dealing with God. And something of this kind happens necessarily and always in the act of loving freedom of real, radical personal communication with one's neighbour. Consequently in the present order of God's saving will, this is always based on God's grace; it is charity.

Whenever a human being in real personal freedom opens his heart to his neighbour, he has already by that very fact done more than simply loved that neighbour, because all that was already encompassed by the grace of God. He has loved his neighbour and in his neighbour he has already loved God. Because he cannot meet his neighbour with love except through the fact that the dynamism of his spiritual freedom supported by the grace of God is already itself always a dynamism towards the unutterable holy mystery which we call God.

This does not mean that love between human beings just as it is usually found is equated with the Christian's explicit love in faith and hope. All we are saying is that genuine love of God is already exercised in it. But this must of course become conscious. It must be such that the goal towards which this love always tends is expressly invoked, named, known, honoured in explicit faith, explicit hope and explicit love. The human love which in its innermost nature is already by God's grace a love of God, must also become explicit love for God who is named, explicitly invoked, religiously sought. This inner dynamism of development is implanted in all love by the grace of God. It has the duty to develop into the explicit specifically Christian character of divine charity. Conversely, it is true for the same reason that this explicit love of God, of the God who is named, although he is not seen, is already intrinsically present in the love of the brother whom we do see. Now it is a fact that there are many people who are redeemed, justified and sanctified by God's grace, although they do not know this. It is also the case that what we as Christians believe, hope and thankfully proclaim of ourselves, is something which is present as an offer in all human beings through God's supernatural, free, unmerited grace. In fact of course, it can also be present as accepted even though many think they are not Christians and not believers. In the depth of their being they can nevertheless be so, and particularly if they really succeed wholeheartedly and with utter unselfishness in loving the brother whom they see. Whether they do this, we of course do not know. We actually do not know it about ourselves either. We of course endeavour in our activity and our lives to love God and our neighbour and both in one. God's judgment alone will decide whether we really summon up this ultimate strength by the efficacious grace of God or whether all that we do is ultimately merely a specious façade behind which a profound, unacknowledged egoism prevails. But we have begun to endeavour to love God in deed and truth, by trying to love the neighbour. All that we experience thereby, disappointment, toil, fret, is fundamentally only

the way in which we try to contrive to turn from ourselves
to the person of our neighbour and to God.

That is difficult. It is the ultimate reality and the hardest
task of our lives. We can be deceived about it time and time
again. But if we have turned in love from self to our neighbour, we have come to God, not by our strength but by
God's grace. God who, as John says, had loved us so that
we might love our neighbour, has truly laid hold of us, has
torn us as it were from self and has given us what in con-
junction constitutes our eternity, a personal union with
others in which we are also united to God.

It is possible to view the same thing once again from an
entirely different angle.

Jesus says to us, "As you did it to one of the least of these
my brethren, you did it to me". How often we have heard
this statement and used it in pious, edifying talk. But suppose we ask ourselves how Jesus could really say that. Is it
not really just a juridical fiction: I give you credit for it, as
though you had done to me personally what you have done
to the least of these other human beings? No, this saying of
Jesus is not a legal fiction, a moral make-believe, a kind of
compensation. It is truly the case that we meet the incarnate
Word of God in the other human being, because God himself really is in this other. If we love him, if we do not as it
were culpably impede the dynamism of this love and fundamentally turn it back towards ourselves, then there occurs precisely the divine descent into the flesh of man, so
that God is in the place where we are and gazes at us in a
human being. This divine descent continues through us and
it then happens that we, because God loves us, love our
neighbour and have already loved God by the very fact of
loving our neighbour. For, of course, we cannot achieve this
love at all except on the basis of that divine love for us which

in fact made itself our brother. The Christological side, if I may so call it, of our brotherly love would have to be taken really seriously and really realized in life. Where the other human being confronts me, there Christ really is, asking me whether I will love him, the incarnate Word of God, and if I say Yes, he replies that he is in the least of his brethren.

One theological aspect may be added in clarification. If we are to take the Christianity of the Incarnation seriously, it will still be the case in eternity that the incarnate Word of God in his humanity is eternally for us the mediator, the gate, bridge, God's actual concrete form, when we see him face to face. Jesus's humanity is not a barrier between us and the immediate presence of the God of grace. Nor is it something which served to mediate only in time, then to be abolished as it were. We shall always be dealing with the God who himself became man. To all eternity there is no theology that is not anthropology.

Is it not the case that we Christians have perhaps still not sufficiently understood our faith, that the various dogmatic affirmations of our faith, though we profess and accept them, nevertheless lie much too far apart, that we have the impression of living in an endlessly complicated world of propositions, dogmas and precepts? In reality, however, the truth is that God is man—and consequently love of God is love of man and vice versa.

The only condition is that we allow the innermost specific movement of this human love to come to its ultimate radical goal and essential fulfilment. Then where this happens, everything is already present—the whole of Christianity, for there is ultimately only one commandment, just as for the Christian there is only one God, he who in the eternal Word became flesh and dwelt among us and who remains not only yesterday and today, but for ever.

Ultimately we know nothing of God if we know nothing of man, of him whom God himself assumed as his own reality and in whom also the ultimate mystery, the ultimate depth of all humanity is comprised. We can ultimately only express the deepest thing about ourselves if we say that we are the reality which God could and has made most entirely his own. Only if we say that, if as it were we spring from anthropology into theology, have we understood what we ourselves are. And consequently we have only understood ourselves in the activity of our life (and that is the only way we understand ourselves) if we are people who love, if we are human beings who in unselfish love have found other human beings and not, of course, merely here and there in some festive hour, but in the brutal, grey, everyday course of our life. There we find God. And we may certainly say that all prayer, worship, law and institutions of the Church are only secondary means for us to do one thing: to love God and the neighbour. And we cannot love God unless we love him in our neighbour. Where we do that we have already fulfilled the Law, thrown the bond of perfection round our whole life, taken the better way which Paul has shown us. Only if we understand that there is a real ultimate unity between love of God and love of the neighbour do we really understand what Christianity is and what a divinely simple thing it is after all. What is divinely simple has, of course, to be expounded, and our whole catechism with all that it contains is the true and genuine exposition, the articulation, the verbal expression of what at bottom we have already grasped if we love our neighbour.

I finally return to what I tried to suggest at the beginning. How as witnesses to the truth and love of God are we to convince people that what we profess in faith actually exists? God seems remote. But there is one thing we can do, love unselfishly and try to tell men that when they do this they have already begun to love God. We can repeatedly exemplify and demonstrate to them the one possible convincing starting-point for the whole of Christianity: love of the neighbour. If we do that we have done what our life must do and we have borne the first and last fundamental testimony to Christianity. We will still have to say very much more about Christianity in the pulpit and in teaching etc. But if this whole message does not begin with the profession by action and life that we are determined to love our neighbour unselfishly, all we say remains unintelligible. The very first key-word capable of convincing anyone today is missing. If we wish to become messengers of God and his love we must quite simply do one thing: love our neighbour, in our life, in care for him, in patience, forgiveness, toleration. Then we have not only begun to practise authentic Christianity, but we already have it whole and entire in germ and kernel. Out of that it can develop in us and bear witness to God's love in Christ Jesus for us, so that men may believe that God exists because they have experienced his love in the love which those who are his bear towards their fellow-men.

"Forbearing One Another and Forgiving Each Other"

"Put on then, as God's chosen ones, holy and beloved, compassion, kindness, lowliness, meekness, and patience, forbearing one another and, if one has a complaint against another, forgiving each other; as the Lord has forgiven you, so you also must forgive. And above all these put on love, which binds everything together in perfect harmony. And let the peace of Christ rule in your hearts, to which indeed you were called in the one body. And be thankful. Let the word of Christ dwell in you richly, as you teach and admonish one another in all wisdom, and as you sing psalms and hymns and spiritual songs with thankfulness in your hearts to God. And whatever you do, in word or deed, do everything in the name of the Lord Jesus, giving thanks to God the Father through him." (Col 3:12–17.)

We are the community to which Paul is writing. He was writing, of course, to a congregation he did not know, so that he could only say to them what he had to say to all. In the first part of the letter the apostle praises the sublime dignity of the eternal Son of God. As the image of God he is before and above all powers. As risen from the dead he is the beginning of the blessed end of our own history, and the head of the Church which is we who have found in him

God's freedom beyond the reach of all principalities and powers. In the second part of the letter, Paul draws the conclusions from these fundamental facts of our Christian life. And to this part the small section of six verses quoted at the head of our meditation belongs. It is a question of the way we Christians are to live if we are moved by faith in God in Christ.

At first sight everything seems to be very clear and simple in regard to this mode of life of the individual and the congregation. Who can object in principle to the recommendation of heartfelt mercy, kindness, humility, gentleness, patience, tolerance and forgiveness, love, peace, gratitude, mutual support in Christian knowledge through instruction by the words of Christ? These ideals, in principle at least, seem almost obvious ones, humane attitudes which we share with all men of mature experience and good will.

But the situation is very different if we allow ourselves to be really affected by these words, if they penetrate the praiseworthy façade of our ordinary decent attitude. Our name may figure in a list of subscribers to good causes and we may have a flag on our coat that protects us from the further rattle of collecting boxes. But have we compassion in our heart of hearts? We have come to an arrangement for coexistence with those around us because that is the best way for our egoism still to have some chance of success. But do we really and truly possess kindness, humility, meekness, patience? We avoid a collision. But do we bear with one another in such a way that others feel they get help from us to bear the burden of their lives? Have we already silently, but from the heart forgiven anyone who has really wronged us? Do we really love or are we only people who have learnt to be shrewd "realists" who no longer dare to lavish a disappointed heart on others? Has our innermost heart been reduced to dead resignation instead of being enfolded in God's peace which is gay, free, full of life and hope? Are we thankful or are we simply resigned? Do we still contrive to say a kind word to others out of real sympathy with them? Is there any music left in us?

If we really listen to the words of the apostle, deadly fear will overcome us about our own heart; it is petrified, dead, like a vicious brood of vipers in its egotism which is only hidden by the cunning by which we dangerously conceal from ourselves the terrifying pit of our own heart.

Let us re-read the text with this kind of fear. Then we shall suddenly realize that it is not addressed to the ideals of our own heart but aims at giving us from God in Christ what it asks of us. For of course it is addressed to God's elect, holy and beloved; it demands a forgiveness animated by the forgiveness which the Lord has given us; it speaks about God's peace, about the power of the word of Christ, about singing in the spirit of God and about action in the name of the Lord Jesus, that is, by the power and freedom given us by the Lord. The apostle presupposes that what he demands really takes place in the individual and in the congregation, despite our pitiable condition of sinners who perpetually have to make a fresh start. But he knows that what he demands comes from God through his grace in faith; according to him, God effects in us the work of our freedom set free to love.

But where in heaven's name is this work of God and of his powerfully liberating grace lifting us from the pit of our evil heart, powerless and choked with itself? If we ask in this doubting way, if we wish to stand apart from ourselves and God in order to watch—unconcerned—whether God and his Spirit will contrive to redeem us from ourselves, we are already in a false position in which nothing can hap-

pen in us. Grace is only experienced if we do not demand
that it should first present itself to us. We must start ourselves, simply assuming it is there, allowing the precept
"Put on, then, ..." to be addressed to us unconditionally.
We must walk and not ask whether we can walk, take the
leap although we think we shall simply fall into the abyss of
our own powerlessness. We have to toil to force ourselves
to produce the work in an ever-renewed despairing attempt,
and leave it to God to add the true disposition without
which all action would once again be nothing—but still a
nothing which we are capable of performing.

And so the text confronts us as it were for the third time,
and once again assumes the appearance which it seemed to
have at the beginning: a call to humanity and decency,
kindness, patience, peaceableness, the freedom and detachment of an exultant heart and all the other things without
which everyday life becomes entangled in futility. But this
very down-to-earth precept now comes as a word of grace
which gives what it demands, which opens out the commonplace into boundless freedom in which the land of
God's glory is found. It comes as a word of grace which
causes God's own work to be continued in us. But precisely
this word of grace is the sober everyday precept which commands us almost harshly and imperiously to wrest the duty
of every day from our lazy and evil hearts because only if we
do this, do we experience and accept our powerlessness and
the power of the grace of God and through both together
are and become God's chosen ones, holy and beloved.

In this way, however, the text becomes a word of
judgment and of encouragement for us Christians of today
who all live in the diaspora, i.e. among people who think
they cannot acknowledge the Christian message as the light
of their life's way. What have we first and foremost to be in

regard to those people? What is the first testimony which
we owe them if we diaspora Christians are not to be guilty
before God and them? We must stand the test of the everyday life which comes not from us but from God. Precisely
this most obvious thing, which is the most difficult, is
what Paul tells us in this text. We must even do it with the
consciousness that what we do in this way in the name of
Christ is done to us by people who are not Christians or
think they are not. They, by a grace which is hidden from
them and from us, do what we do or should do: show love,
patience, genuine compassion, peace. And this is an indict-
ment, a judgment on us. Only if we are conscious of this can
our action become a true testimony to the power of grace
which operates where it will and is no respecter of persons.

Our heart is weak and cowardly and always overtaxed
by what the word of God demands of us. That word must
give us what it requires of us. That is why we celebrate the
Lord's Supper. We announce his death which redeems us
into the freedom of the children of God. We place ourselves
under the law of his Cross, on which ultimate human powerlessness, obediently in agreement with itself, became an act
manifesting the power of God. We receive the Body of
the Lord which was given for us, so that each who receives
it with faith may not be left alone with his weakness any
more, so that in him too the kindness of the living God may
be effective and grant him to begin the everyday practice of
obvious commonplace duty. In this everyday duty, provided
it is accepted quite unconditionally, death is present in an
inner way that can easily be overlooked. For there is un-
rewarded sacrifice there, absolutely silent renunciation, the
hazardous enterprise that demands all and apparently gives
nothing. There, in other words, is death, renunciation,
silent acceptance. A person to whom it is given to do and

suffer this, from a source which he does not know, dies with Christ whether he knows it or not. Because we know this in faith, we celebrate the Lord's Supper, in which he himself accepted his death. It is a terrible thing to place oneself under the Cross of him who expressed the ultimate when he commended his life into the hands of him whom he called the God who had forsaken him. But there alone is the burning bush of redemption and love.

ONE SPIRIT, MANY GIFTS

Pagan Christians and Christian Pagans

Matthew 8:1–13

The Lord was sent in the first instance to the lost sheep of the house of Israel. This nation had been the chosen people, the people of God's Covenant, the possession of his Father. When the Son came into his own home, however, his own people did not receive him. The "patriotism" of this nation was to have consisted of faith in God and his word and also in his new Word. But the incarnate Word did not meet with such faith. That nation considered that its relations with God were long since finally settled and that there was no further alteration to be made in them; it thought that its Covenant with God was a reason for not having him come any nearer, that its earlier obedience dispensed it from listening any further to what God might wish to say. With the nation of faith in the Father, the Son found no faith, because it already had too much "faith". He found faith in a centurion of the pagan occupying power. Then even he who already knows all was filled with wonder. His whole life long that astonishment accompanied the heart of the Son of man, the emotion prompted by the fact that many who seem to be outside are within, while the native citizens of the Kingdom are cast into the outer darkness; that unconditional faith often comes more readily from the heart of the "unbeliever" than from those who have always been orthodox, and that heaven finds true penance among sinners rather than among those who think they have no need of it.

All this still holds good today. The frontiers of the Kingdom of God do not simply coincide with the dividing lines between the denominations or between practising and non-practising Catholics. Not that it is not God's will for one to be a Catholic and a practising one at that. But among these Catholics not all are truly children of the Kingdom. The book of life is not simply identical with denominational statistics, parish records and the membership lists of Catholic confraternities.

We must constantly remind ourselves of this, obvious though it may be—in theory and in general. Not everyone who says Lord, Lord, enters the Kingdom of heaven. The Catholic whose practice is really sufficient for the Kingdom of heaven has to practise not only in Church but also in life, and he has in fact to practise patience, an unassuming spirit, love of his neighbour, honesty and all those virtues in which the children of the world often seem to be superior to us. Orthodoxy and the faith which truly justifies are two different things. Someone with "a clean slate" may have a heart that lacks God and real love. Church-going is not in itself true Christianity. In fact orthodoxy, respectability and fidelity to the Church can present the danger of self-right-eousness and pious hypocrisy. Everyone hides a certain amount of faulty intention somewhere or other behind his good work. We perhaps admit our failure, but only on condition that others do not take our admission literally. If we are good we make it a reason why we don't need to improve. We belong to the people who fill the confessionals; they think that if they have once confessed a fault they no longer need discard it. We make sacrifices, but mostly they are only a fee exempting us from those we really ought to make. When a call to penance is made, we take it as referring to others, not to ourselves. If our conscience is too uneasy we preach amendment to others. In short, in some respects we are all pagan Christians who refuse our Lord faith. The Lord is still walking among his people and cannot but be astonished at how little faith he finds.

We ought to keep a look out for the "Christian pagans", i.e. people who are near to God without realizing it, but from whom the light is hidden by the shadow which *we* throw. From East and West men are entering the Kingdom of God by roads which are not shown on any official map. When we meet them they ought to be able to see from us that the official paths on which we are travelling are safer and shorter.

The Prophetic Person and the Church

The Church perpetually faces new tasks. Those created for it by the change in the historical situation, those that God himself sets because he wishes the Church to grow and display the wealth of its hidden life in ever new forms and patterns. Now the human beings who first perceive these new tasks, call for action to meet them, master them in an exemplary way, are certainly not always the officially appointed pastors of the Church, the bishops and popes. The impulse to new vital movements originating in God's providence operating in the Church can also start and in fact perpetually does start from the "little ones" in God's Kingdom, the uneducated and the poor, obscure people who pray and do penance, in short, from "prophetic" persons who, moved by the "Spirit who breathes where he will", address the message of their life, their example and their words to the Church.

When God's Spirit raises up such persons, a special mutual relation arises between them and the Church. On the one hand the Church may not "extinguish the spirit" of these men. The Church, including its official pastors, must hear their message. It must pray to have such prophetic persons. It must receive from them the keyword as it were of what is to be done precisely now at this particular moment in history.

This is what has happened time and time again. Innumerable examples might be quoted. Benedict of Nursia, for example, was not a priest and yet by the pneuma (spirit) of his wisdom and discretion he became the father of monasticism, and safely guided the Church and the culture of antiquity into the new era of the Middle Ages. The nun Juliana of Liège died having to all appearances had no success with her mission, yet gave the decisive impetus for the introduction of the feast of Corpus Christi. The powerful Pope Innocent III saw in a dream that a poor man, Francis of Assisi, was the decisive support of the Church. And it was not merely a dream. How many others without office or position, powerful only by their spirit, does the history of the Church record as agents or inspirers of new vital movements and of epoch-making decisions: Antony and Pacomius, the fathers of monasticism, Catherine of Siena who ended the Avignon Captivity of the popes, Joan of Arc, Teresa of Avila, the great teacher of all modern mysticism, Mary Ward the patient champion of the modern type of religious order for women, Margaret Mary Alacoque the prophetess of devotion to the Sacred Heart of Jesus, Bernadette Soubirous of Lourdes etc.

On the other hand, however, even such prophetic persons are individual members of the Church; their gift of grace is always only a limited segment of the many gifts of grace which the one Spirit distributes among the members of the Church. Consequently it must allow full scope to other gifts in other people. And, it must not be forgotten, prudent criticism, sober theological reflection, a perception of the dangers of onesidedness and narrow views can be gifts of the Spirit in the Church. Prophetic individuals must remain subject in obedience to the teaching and pastoral office of the official Church. Whether or not they do so willingly, confidently and unreservedly is precisely the touchstone which shows whether the spirit of these men is really from God. When someone is genuinely moved by the Spirit of God, he is humble, afraid of error, and acknowledges that in the long run it is only through the teaching and pastoral office of the Church and through the healthy instinct of the whole Church that he is preserved from the danger of presenting his own very human, even if very pious, spirit as the Holy Spirit.

There is really no lack of examples of the importance of such criticism of prophetic individuals by the Church. The "visions" of St Hildegard of Bingen, of St Elizabeth of Schönau, of St Bridget of Sweden, St Frances of Rome and others, are mixed with strange errors which these canonized and beatified persons nevertheless thought to be revealed and sometimes tried to impose on their contemporaries, including the bishops, in very authoritative-sounding terms. St Bernard of Clairvaux prophesied the success of the Second Crusade which he inspired, yet himself lived to see it fail. How often at critical moments in the Church's history (about the year 1000, at the end of the Middle Ages, when an end was put to the States of the Church etc.) have prophecies about the future been current, which were not fulfilled. In his testament to his sons, St Francis imposed a command which he intended to be strictly binding, that no explanations were to be added to his Rule and no papal declarations of its meaning were to be requested, and by this he provoked a severe crisis in his young order. This was only overcome through the wisdom and courage of St Antony who, despite his father's testament, asked the pope for an interpretation of the Rule. The great apostle of eastern Germany, Norbert

of Xanten († 1134) thought he knew by revelation that
Anti-Christ would appear in his own lifetime, despite what
St Bernard had to say to the contrary. St Catherine of Siena
believed it had been revealed to her that the blessed Virgin
had not been conceived immaculate. St Vincent Ferrer
(† 1419) proclaimed the imminent end of the world,
appealing to a revelation and to the miracles worked by him.
Blessed Alanus of Rupe († 1475) a great advocate of the
Rosary, announced the most impossible fantasies (e. g. about
the origin of the Rosary in apostolic times) as revelations
imparted to him. "All these things", he said, "I attest and
swear to by my faith in the Blessed Trinity. May I be accursed
if I have swerved from the path of truth." Yet he did err and
is not accursed. The "great promise" of St Margaret Mary,
in the form in which the saint communicated it as revelation,
is open to not inconsiderable objections in the judgment of
grave theologians. St Catherine Labouré, the visionary who
propagated the "miraculous medal" also reported revelations which, as she herself honestly and humbly recognized,
proved to be erroneous. Even certain particular predictions
(about the end of the world war etc.) and theological expressions of the children of Fatima give cause for justified
reserve, even though they do not affect the essential of the
message of Fatima.

These and other examples of the kind are ample evidence
how even holy people who have brought rich blessings to
the Church by their charismata are only human, liable to
error and partly dependent on the spirit of their age, unable
of themselves alone clearly to distinguish between the
inspirations of the Holy Spirit and their own contributions.
It is only the Spirit in the Church's official ministry which
makes this possible for them. This difficulty of "discernment of spirits" (which is a gift of God's grace) must not

make us impatient and hasty. Neither credulity nor hidden or open hostility to new effects of prophetic spirit in the Church is the correct attitude. Just as we must respond to the admonition to prayer and penance, which is of course ultimately the only too well justified kernel of the most recent revelations, and which can never be repeated too often, so too it would be a sign of our lack of the necessary spirit of discernment of spirits if we were to reject as unbelieving rationalism every warning to be cautious and to avoid onesidedness, every lengthy testing by the Church, every investigation of new revelations according to the sober criterion of sound theology and psychology. There are sufficient events recently to suggest the need for caution and scrutiny of this kind, and also sufficient people among the pious who need to be told that obedience to the Church and even instruction by sober theology is an essential mark of whether the spirit of which they wish to promote recognition in the Church is really from God. Only through incorporation into the Church is there any guarantee that the "prophetic" activity of those called to it will really bear fruit.

Do Not Evade Decisions!

In Christian life today we have many principles, general norms and few prescriptions, directions and instructions for the concrete situation. Not that there can be too many principles. When they are correct, there can never be too many of them, and it is right to proclaim them. It is also evident that a lot of things would be much improved if the principles that are proclaimed were followed and that the principles are not proved false because their rejection brings misfortune. Yet those who proclaim the principles should surely also ponder why these principles when preached are so little heeded. If they answer, because it is the hour of darkness and of the power of evil, they should also ask themselves why the latter is supposed suddenly to be stronger than previously and why the "ancient truths" and "unchanging principles" are of less avail. If they explain, as is after all of greater practical importance and more correct, that the historical changes of the times with their new conditions have created new problems and difficulties which can only be overcome slowly and patiently, then they must ask themselves whether they know how these new conditions and situations are to be given shape and form so as to provide a tolerable milieu for the realization of those principles, or whether once again they would only have general principles available instead of prescriptions. Viewed in this way it is clear that the more doctrinal proclamation of general principles ought to be accompanied by a statement of prescriptions.

At the same time it must be made plain that these prescriptions themselves cannot consist of principles, as is the case in our preaching and teaching, in the position adopted by the Church and by Christians in regard to concrete questions and decisions in the life of the individual and the nation. That is why what we say often sounds well-worn and familiar, tedious, facile and almost hollow. In itself it is not. For principles must be proclaimed. But people are mostly on the look-out for prescriptions and spontaneously take this proclamation to be intended to announce prescriptions, as indeed it is often wrongly supposed by the speakers themselves to be doing. People are quite right, really, to have this expectation. For the hearers are supposed to act, that is, to do something concrete, for that is the only way fundamentals and essentials and eternal truths can be carried into effect. But what they mostly hear is the ideal instead of the actual model, the abstract proposition instead of a vividly depicted actual example. Consequently we give the impression of wanting to restore the past—and even defend this by urging that the time for the "movements" of the twenties is now passed. Our pronouncements seem too cautious, anxiously decanted, measured out. It is all very correct, but rather sterile. No one clear unmistakable note. Too much golden mean. The cart is right out in the middle of the road, well away from either ditch, but it doesn't move on. People are proud of the Catholic synthesis of principles that are difficult to harmonize and that sometimes seem almost incompatible. But it is easy to lose sight of the question how this balanced system of carefully reconciled principles actually looks in fact. With the best will in the world, not all the actual features of our general view of things that have to be taken into account can be fully brought out to the same extent. A decision has to be taken to present it in a quite definite style.

For it is not the case that men with their limitations can decide from one single principle all that they have to do and carry into effect, however much they may strive to integrate the multiplicity of their nature, their tasks and principles in ever higher and richer unifying principles. Inevitably a man has a plurality of principles. To respect them simultaneously is only possible by a decision, and for this, prescriptions are needed. Yet these are often lacking, or only the old ones are proffered, and they have already turned into abstract principles or become false, that is, historically ineffectual. Eyes are on the good old days, which of course could scarcely have given birth to the present if they had been as ideal as all that. We cannot undertake here to give more detailed grounds for our assertion of the lack of practical prescriptions in present-day Catholicism in Germany. But to be honest we must admit that the mood in the Christian camp is dull, rather bored, listless. They don't even have any proper disputes among themselves. Unity is preserved, but preferably by avoiding ticklish questions. Things are smoothed over and settled by administrative procedures and the problems are supposed to be solved. It is not so easy to make clear to the ordinary man anything really new that we want (apart from the maintenance of things as they are, certain difficult moral requirements and the rejection of communism), how we envisage the future, not the one which is just coming—"The future has already begun"—

but the future that we will to come, work for and fight for. If anyone feels obliged to contradict this, he can regard the present writer as one such ordinary person, and realize from his case that there do seem to be people all the same whom the practical prescriptions have not yet reached sufficiently clearly.

If one thinks, for example, of recent Catholic congresses, one might say with a certain amount of malicious exaggeration, knowing that there are, of course, other quite different sides to these gatherings as well, that a few years ago people still wanted something definite, but now they are more cautious: they want principles to be carried out. In terms of the Spiritual Exercises of St Ignatius one might say that they choose the abstract end, instead of racking their brains and, even more important, rending their heart over the choice of concrete means to the attainment of a provisional, of course, but quite definite goal. Let us hope the day is still distant when people say, "Such and such people in those days at least knew what they were after", or when from sheer boredom and weariness of being free and available for anything, without any binding prescription, people submit to the yoke of men who possess prescriptions even if they are false and short-sighted ones. It almost looks as if people in countries in Eastern Europe, perhaps only a small part of them but all the more valuable a part, are slowly ceasing for these and similar reasons, to envy us in the West. Yet we are moving towards such new and difficult possibilities that it should stimulate the hard thinkers and strong hearts among Christians, each in his own domain, to possess not only abstract principles but also practical prescriptions, not merely a Catholic faith but also a Christian view of things, if we understand by this not the bare sum-total of correct principles, particularly of natural law, but an organized body of correct and historically appropriate practical prescriptions.

Christians in the last few centuries have come to represent the conservative principle, though that is really not something that should be taken for granted. It is not surprising, therefore, that they consider the maxims by which they in fact live as too self-evident to require much detailed discussion, or that they hold up as a reproach to their iconoclastic opponents the abiding principles. For they can demonstrate these with certainty and think, but not with quite as much certainty, that they have thereby defended the old maxims and prescriptions. Christians are on the defensive and that tempts them to defend themselves from their strongest positions. Now it is easier to cast doubt on prescriptions than on principles. Furthermore we have already seen that the Church has not in most cases the task and authority to lay down these prescriptions. Naturally it has to proclaim, for example, the fundamental moral principles of any economic system but not to recommend a particular model for a more effective economic system than the one we have. The official representatives of the Church are aware of this with greater or less degrees of clarity. The Church has already had unfortunate experiences with the recommendation or defence of particular prescriptions and maxims, the alliance of Throne and Altar, for example, and has learnt caution, is afraid of saying things that would have to be withdrawn later. So there is a retreat into principles.

But that does not mean that Christians and especially the Christian laity (who are also the Church), are dispensed from the task of having prescriptions and maxims of a kind that are compatible with the Gospel and the Church's teaching and at the same time form a concrete programme

of Christian activity. Simply because the Church cannot
supply them ready-made and ready for use, it is far from the
case that Christians can have a clear conscience even if they
have not got such maxims, or that they cannot be morally
reproached in this regard by the Church, even though direct
ecclesiastical censure can, in most cases, only be directed
against actions that contradict principles but not against
false prescriptions or the lack of any in the life of the
individual or the community. For example, it is only very
indirectly or not at all that the Church can dissuade from a
mistaken choice of profession or marriage, although this
can be much more devastating than a sin, against which the
Church does protest. One might express it fairly accurately
by saying that the finding and disseminating of prescriptions
is first and last a matter for the laity and for the apostolate
that is theirs, the action of Catholics, as distinct from
"Catholic Action". Here they do not and cannot simply
take their orders from the hierarchy. They should not
expect orders of that kind and should not think that the
apostolate of the laity only begins at the point where such
commands or particular wishes are expressed, in Catholic
Action, for example. Here they can usually expect no direct
mandate from the Church but certainly from their conscience and from God. The distinction between principles
and prescriptions could perhaps also help to settle the
question of the position and function of the layman in the
Church, in the lay apostolate and of the difference between
Catholic Action and the activities of Catholics as Catholics.
If Christian lay people find and put into effect these appropriate and well-timed prescriptions, the Church (or Christendom) is operative in them, for of course they are also of the
Church, yet the Church does not need to commit itself in its
authoritative teaching and pastoral office. But it has to

ensure, for example, that Christians do not think that they have fulfilled their duties if they are living in peace with the authoritatively proclaimed principles of the Church.

Lay people should be encouraged and educated much more than formerly to discern the will of God even in spheres where the Church cannot tell them what it is in its actual individual detail. They should be made aware that we Christians can have a duty sometimes to unite (even perhaps at the cost of sacrifice and mental self-denial), not only on principles but also on a prescription, a practical proposition, even if this cannot authoritatively be imposed by the Church's magisterium. We should learn that it may be wiser tactics to work out a few prescriptions than always to proclaim all the correct principles all together. That supplies the humility for courage to be healthily "one-sided", for it is easier by the nature of the case then to blame oneself than when one is the representative of principles. We might be more serene, more confident and have more enthusiasm and sense of mission in representing practical prescriptions than we commonly are except when the big speeches are being made. The self-assurance of the followers of Moral Rearmament might to some extent be an example. Practical prescriptions can only flourish in minds and hearts where there is proper freedom of opinion and inquiry, speech and discussion. According to Pius XII, there must be a public opinion in the Church because the lack of it would be harmful to flock and shepherd. One may well think that it is not very lively, though there are gratifying exceptions. The only defence of the inheritance of the past is the conquest of the future. But for that we need, as well as much else that is far more important, practical prescriptions, not only abstract principles.

The Christian in the World according to the Fathers

The question has perpetually to be raised how the Christian in the "world" can realize the ideals of Christianity in his life. It is a vital question which has to be re-experienced and mastered afresh because the Christian layman has to combine the ethos of his secular profession with the other-worldly calling which is in Christ Jesus. His profession summons him to the difficulties and satisfaction of an earthly task which must be taken seriously so that his heart is in it. His Christian vocation commands him to seek what is above, to consider himself a stranger on this earth and thoroughly to realize that the pattern of this world passes away and that it profits nothing to gain the whole world, if for the sake of it one loses one's soul.

The early Christian took the attitude of watching for the coming of the Lord so much for granted that in all the writings of the Fathers we find only a few works which expressly deal with the problem of lay asceticism. All the greater importance attaches therefore to the writings in which Clement of Alexandria aimed at promoting mutual contact between the Christian mind and the cultural life of antiquity. We must recall the ascetic seriousness of the early Christian ideal of perfection if we are to realize the magnitude of such an endeavour which, while maintaining the fundamental attitude of Christianity, expressly aimed at tracing the ideal pattern of the Christian in the world.

The situation at that time was a special one, and for long after none would be equally favourable to such an enterprise. Christianity was stronger at the end of the second and beginning of the third century and its followers were more numerous. It could therefore no longer escape the question of its relation to civilization, learning etc. On the other hand the idealism of the early Church was still alive and this demanded the highest of every Christian. The age of mass Christianity after Constantine had not yet dawned, when the Christian ideals almost inevitably took refuge in monastic circles. There they were developed and given a monastic stamp. In that form they were then to dominate and determine for long centuries the ideals of Christian perfection even of the laity, and even in the Third Order movements of the Middle Ages. Clement was ideally suited to the task. He was a much-travelled, well-read city-dweller familiar with the religious trends of his age and (as at least appears very likely) the father of a family.

Clement's aim is clear even in the formal structure and literary character of the great trilogy he planned: *Hortatory Address to the Greeks,* the *Tutor,* and *Miscellanies.* The third of these is to be regarded either as the projected Teacher or as a work preparatory to it; the point is of no special importance for our present purpose. The pagan's conversion to Christianity *(Hortatory Address)* is followed by the moral formation of the Christian by the Logos as his pedagogue *(Tutor)* and then by his spiritual education by the Logos as teacher *(Miscellanies).* The moral formation in the *Tutor,* however, as its whole contents show, is concerned with the rich, cultivated, married citizen of one of the great cities of that age, a man surrounded by his family, his household and his public profession. Clement aims at making him a perfect Christian in the actual circumstances of his life. His further development in the *Miscellanies* into a "gnostic" also concerns the same person in precisely the same conditions. Moreover, while the spiritual formation in the *Miscellanies* builds all the time on the faith of simple Christianity—all "gnostic" perfection is only intended to be a development of what faith already contains in out-line—nevertheless the "gnostic" includes among his aims the cultivation of philosophy, music, dialectic, astrology; he reads poets and philosophers. We could say that gnosis as Clement understands it is the total formation of the personality directed towards supernatural union with God and incorporating in its ideal all the natural values. "There is only one way of truth, but in it the streams flow together from different sides as though into an eternal river" (*Strom.* I, 5, 29,1). The *Miscellanies* keep on returning to the prob-lems of the *Tutor,* and this shows that while for Clement the "gnostic" is the ideal goal of his Christian, the vital centre of his preoccupations is the moral formation of the layman, which is the subject of the *Tutor.* The Christian in the world is therefore his essential theme. The literary form of his works corresponds to this intention of integrating the world through the perfect Christian layman. Clement is the first Christian to write "literature of a secular kind, a literature of the same kind as that of the cultivated Greco-Roman world of that time" (C. A. Bernoulli). In his thought and writing he was entirely a cultivated person of that age, at home in its literature, philosophy and ideals and yet a Christian. From all this, the task which Clement set himself is evident: the question of the lay Christian and of lay per-fection, the integration of the world in Christian personal life.

We shall examine more closely this problem and Clement's attempt at a solution. But we are not concerned with all the details of his solution, nor the extent of his success. Only the attitude Clement adopts can be an example to us today, not his solution. His world and ours are too different for more to be possible.

Clement seeks a solution which leaves intact the eschatological ethos of Christianity; for him too the martyr is the perfect Christian. Virginity is the "better choice" and takes precedence of matrimony in the perspective of salvation. (We cannot go into the question here to what extent all his statements about marriage are consistent with this.) Clement also seems to have written a separate work in praise of continence. He adopts the same attitude to real poverty.

The fundamental question for Clement and his view of it begins to appear, however, when he distinguishes between the innermost Christian attitude in these active expressions of Christian perfection (martyrdom, virginity, poverty) and the performances themselves. He sees that the essential in these typical achievements of Christian perfection is in a way located behind them, that it can indeed be manifested and find expression but is not simply identical with them, that in fact it is even possible for there to be a gap between the interior disposition and the performances themselves. Consequently the Christian attitude can also find a real and tangible expression in a secular life. He knows that we should be martyrs in *everything,* by suffering, but also in all our actions. It is that attitude, and in particular love, which makes a man a martyr by making him renounce self-will for the will of God, and bear witness to God. Conversely, even the external achievement of physical martyrdom as such is not for Clement an unambiguous criterion of perfection. Similarly he is aware that celibacy can lead to aridity of soul.

Without holy knowledge the unmarried can come to hate humanity and be bereft of all love.

On this basis Clement now seeks to work out positively the Christian meaning of a secular life, i.e. not merely to show that a secular life is tolerated and permissible, to what extent and in what way, but to show that it positively possesses a Christian and moral significance which can make a human being perfect.

And so "no other writer of antiquity ... discusses the question of the moral significance of earthly possessions in such detail as Clement" (Bardenhewer). For the first time in Christian literature he refers in this connection to social points of view. Property well employed is a means of linking people more closely together, it forms and sustains society. For him, rich and poor are not at all directly important religious categories. Clement regards married life in the same spirit. Here, too, it is not a question for him simply of the moral legitimacy of matrimony as opposed to Gnostic views hostile to marriage. Even though he did not wholly succeed in reconciling the Christian meaning of marriage with Christian esteem for virginity, this is pardonable because of the intention which guided him in his praise of matrimony, and he makes up for it by pitching the moral requirements for marriage too high rather than too low. We do not need to go into details here either. What is important is the principle of his endeavour, his determination to regard marriage in the light of the principle that we bear witness to the Lord by our whole life. "We must be holy, not only in spirit but also in our whole conduct, way of life and body" (*Strom.* III, 6, 47, 1). The decisive thing here is that this is not directed against the Libertines, but against the Encratites. The holiness which bears witness to the Lord is therefore regarded not so much as consisting in domination over the body but in its intrinsic reality and activity as holiness. "We enjoy the creation with all thankfulness and with our mind fixed on what is lofty." "Created is celibacy, created is the world. Both can give thanks in the position which they have received, if they know for what purpose they received it." "Marriage to a wife founds a house of the Lord" (*Strom.* III, 14, 95, 3; 18, 105, 1; 18, 108, 2).

Clement surveys the whole civilization of his age: baths and sports, clothing, jewellery, unguents and garlands, laughter, speech, household furniture, attendance at dinner parties, eating and drinking, sleep, footwear, beauty, trade etc. These themes are sufficient in themselves to show that Clement is concerned with the intrinsic christianization of life in the world. Everywhere he shows that he is conscious of the freedom of the Christian man. It is not that the Christian leaves the world in its worldly state; knowing that he is not of the world, he must nevertheless not abandon the world to itself out of his own lofty freedom and spirituality, but must bring it back to God. For it is the creation of the self-same God who set up the Cross in the world.

Clement was well aware what he was aiming at. A remark of his shows this. The true gnostic, the perfect Christian that is, is "of the world and above the world". For Clement, only those are pious "who serve God well and faultlessly in human things" (*Strom.* VII, 1, 3, 4). The perfect Christian is not only of the world, but neither is he above the world merely in the Gnostic sense that everything which is not "pneumatic" is condemned. The Christian is both. In this way Clement has expressed the metaphysical formula of Christian personal life, its age-old problem which has to be solved afresh in every age.

Clement's attempt is unique in patristic literature by its explicitness and breadth. The great Origen himself is already much less world-affirming and optimistic. Himself an ascetic, he already lays the intellectual foundation of the ideals of the coming monasticism. The second half of the third century is quite generally a remarkably unfruitful period in patristic literature. In the first half of the fourth century the magnificent flowering of monasticism then begins in the midst of the imperial Church when the level of the masses was sinking. Starting in Egypt, it soon covered the whole of the East, and from the second half of the fourth century onwards decisively influenced the Church of the West also.

We need not here discuss the causes which led to this rapid and splendid development of monasticism, which alone really transformed into an "order" the Church's ascetics and virgins. In the first three centuries they had lived unassumingly among the local congregations. Then monasticism transmitted its form of life, to a large extent at any rate, to the clergy. In these two ways the Christian laity was marked off as a separate part of the people of God, not only from the hierarchical point of view of the Church's constitution but also from the point of view of the ideals of Christian life. This development took place very quickly. When Chrysostom preached about the perfection of Christian life his hearers retorted: After all we are not monks! So even then the laity felt themselves, though wrongly, to be a part of Christendom which is less strictly bound to the ideals of Christianity. Conversely, Christian perfection and monasticism were almost identified.

For Basil, monk and Christian are almost identical concepts. When Chrysostom wants to extol the ideals of a perfect Christian marriage, he can find no higher praise than to say it is scarcely inferior to the life of the monk. The parable of the thirty-fold, sixty-fold and hundred-fold fruit is to our way of thinking applied too simply to the following

Christian states of life: marriage, widows, virgins. When Jerome writes about girls' education, it turns into a set of instructions for the education of a future nun. In the *Celestial Hierarchy* of the Pseudo-Areopagite, the monks occupy a special place before the rest of the laity. In the pilgrim story when some holy monk or other receives the revelation that he is not more perfect than a certain modest layman in his hidden holiness, it is nevertheless mostly the case (with one laudable exception) that the layman in question finally becomes a monk or a nun, in other words, becomes outwardly what in the eyes of the author of the story he already was at heart. In biographies such as that of the younger Melania or in the story of Nilus of Sinai, the happy ending to a Christian marriage is for husband and wife to enter the cloister. For Augustine, not to mention Jerome, the laity are rather too obviously the weaker brethren. As we have said, we cannot here inquire more precisely and distinguish to what extent such views simply express in a still rather undifferentiated way the Christian truth of faith that the ascetic life is superior to secular life as a state, not as a moral evaluation of the individual with his perhaps real vocation to a secular life. Nor can we inquire how far they expressed a genuine picture of actual conditions. How far did they derive not from Christian conviction but from the pessimism of later antiquity and from Hellenistic hostility to the body? This had always regarded the "spirit" and its ascent as more Christian (and monasticism, of course, was a "philosophy"). At all events the facts show that at the height of the patristic period the ideals of the Christian in the world were regarded in the light of those of monasticism. Consequently not everything possible was done to develop a lay morality and lay perfection, and reflection on the specifically Christian values of secular life still left much to be desired.

We do not wish to imply by this that the golden age of Christian monasticism in antiquity only had the effect of impeding the conscious development of lay perfection. That would be onesided, even if we leave entirely out of account the question how far the need for such a thing was felt at that time at all. Monasticism indubitably had the highest possible degree of influence in preserving and promoting the vitality of Christian ideals generally. In that way it certainly exercised an educative influence on lay Christianity. The radical way in which its numerous holy representatives gave an example of Christian living to a tired and aging civilization could only be beneficial to the great mass of average Christians. When opposition to ascetic ideals sprang up, a tendency of hostility to monasticism can be seen at least as much in clerical circles as among the laity. Such opposition was therefore not strictly a lay matter. The greatest service imaginable was rendered to the civilization and ethos of the lay Christian by the fact that monasticism gave to the world of antiquity the example of a life of manual labour and showed this to be an integral part of the ideal Christian life. Augustine's book *On the Work of the Monks* is the first patristic eulogy of manual work in contrast to the contemptuous view of such a life current in antiquity.

Apart from all this, however, we find in the main patristic period sufficient indications that it was not forgotten that the layman too, like every Christian, is called to perfection and can and must realize it in his own particular way. A few examples must be quoted.

Lay people who were martyrs do not directly concern our question, of course, for they were saints because martyrs, and in the perfection of martyrdom all differences of state of life disappear. But at least a word or two must be devoted to them. Among them we find soldiers and artisans, doctors, philosophers, married couples, mothers with their children, great ones of the earth and slaves. They all testify by their very existence that those who are great in the Kingdom of God are chosen from all conditions and professions and that they had therefore already sanctified themselves in their secular state. Sometimes this is expressly attested of these people who bore witness in their blood. Among these are the holy martyrs Crispin and Crispianus the shoemakers who were full of social spirit and readiness to help, and the hard-working gardener Phocas of Sinope. The excellent workmanship of the *quattro coronati* is expressly extolled; it was the result of the Christian ethos of their work. In one ancient account of a martyr's life we significantly read: *statio artis facta est domus orationis.* The numerous holy doctors honoured as *anargyroi,* giving treatment free, can only be mentioned in passing.

In antiquity there were very few known saints who were and remained lay people, as compared with the number of holy bishops, priests, monks and virgins known to us. A few holy artisans and doctors, about whom we know little except their sanctity and their profession, though this has its importance. A few fathers and mothers honoured as saints or renowned for their holiness, to whom attention was drawn by a great son, like Monica, Augustine's mother, the parents and grandparents of St Basil, St John Chrysostom's mother, and finally saints who because of their exemplary life as laymen were made bishops. This need not surprise us. By the nature of the case the ideal of sanctity at that time was still, and rightly, strongly orientated (but a little too directly) by the ideal of the martyr. It is therefore understandable that a parallel to the holy witnesses was first and foremost seen in the life of a hermit and monk. His asceticism was of course expressly regarded as a substitute for martyrdom. It is hardly surprising either that in addition attention was still primarily fixed on the religious leaders of the people, the bishops, especially as at that time a religiously important personality, whatever his profession in life, and even if he were married, was more easily made a bishop than would be the case today. We need only recall Gregory the wonder-worker, Ambrose, Paulinus of Nola, Martin of Tours, Parthenius of Lampsacus etc.

Not only where shining examples in actual reality imposed it, but in theory also it was never entirely forgotten that there can and must be sanctity in the world. We have already mentioned the pilgrim story which appears with a number of variants in monastic literature. Read and endlessly reread, it must have maintained the realization that "Truly whether virgin or married woman, whether monk or layman, God gives the Holy Spirit to each according to his own good pleasure" (*Vitae Patrum* VI, 3 n. 17).

John Chrysostom is the preacher of Christian lay perfection. Though he was also one of the most ardent promoters of monasticism, he never forgot that every Christian must become perfect. He was angered by hearing time and time again the same facile phrase in objection to his sermons on the ideals of Christian life: "After all we are not monks". Ascetic and Christian in the world are both subject to the same law of Christ. The Sermon on the Mount is addressed to all. The married Christian in the world can practise virtue just as the monk can, can pray and read scripture (a favourite theme of the great preacher), in short, can be a Christian equally with the monk. For the moral value of a life is ultimately determined by love, and without it even poverty and martyrdom are useless. Christian perfection essentially consists in perfect love which springs from true faith and works itself out in a life in accordance with God's commandments. That is a programme which is the same for all. Concern for the perfection of all, for a holiness which is not the monopoly of any state of life, occupied Chrysostom all his life. For an idea of his ideal of marriage, for example, his 20th Homily on the Letter to the Ephesians may be referred to; it contains a whole code of Christian marriage.

Mention must finally be made of patristic correspondence. This shows that even at that time spiritual letters were written "from soul to soul", to lay people who wanted to live Christianity perfectly. Only a few letters are involved, it is true, and by the nature of the case they are almost always addressed to persons in high positions with whom the letter-writer had some personal connection. Mostly they are answers to queries, letters of thanks or admonitions. Their purely circumstantial origin means that only particular sections of the spiritual life are dealt with in these letters of spiritual direction. They are not concerned to describe the interior spiritual attitude of the Christian, or to lay its theological foundations. Everything concerning principles is for the most part taken for granted as known, and instruction only deals with the way in which faith must be applied at the relevant points in practical life. We should look in vain in these letters for a theoretical presentation of lay asceticism as a whole or its various domains. Occasionally however we do find not only valuable warnings and suggestions, but quite detailed instructions on married life, prayer and other special questions of the kind which will always arise for a zealous Christian who tries to put his faith into practice. Rich experience of life, theological wisdom and a lofty personal ethos find expression in the words of these letters which will remain interesting evidence of ancient Christian piety and a source of valuable stimulus.

The Divine Mystery of Marriage

"This mystery is great, but I say it in regard to Christ and the Church" (Eph 5:32). Catholic literature and preaching on marriage in the last few decades has untiringly quoted and expounded this remark of the apostle. But it has been and is mostly a question of simply transferring the mystery: Christ—Church to the mutual relation and loving unity of husband and wife. It has not been shown more precisely how in this mystery the dynamism of love on the human level and that of God's love from on high come together, how the former flows into the heart of God while the second pours into the hearts of human beings.

Even by the standards of human experience the holy and bold undertaking of beginning one united life of love and fidelity reaches out into the mystery of God. For a man to dispose of himself entirely in the fundamental freedom of his human reality, and to dare to entrust himself, his heart, life, lot and eternal dignity as a person to another human being and thereby commit himself to what is after all ultimately the mysteriously new, unknown and unfathomable mystery of another person, is something which can only be done in the highest venture of love and trust. And viewed from outside it may often take place in a way which makes it seem an everyday and quite commonplace business. Nevertheless, it is in reality what it appears to the lovers to be: the always unique wonder of love. And that borders on God. For it comprises the whole man and his whole destiny. Anything of that kind, however, deliberately performed, always means coming into God's presence, whether people realize this or not. It always involves the perhaps unmentioned, silent partner, encompassing all, saving and blessing, whom we call God. For such an undertaking has no limits, points to the limitless and unconditional, and is only possible in the boundless scope of the spiritual person, which is orientated towards God. In truly personal love there is always an unconditional element implied which points beyond the contingence of the lovers themselves. If they truly love, they continually develop above and beyond themselves. They enter into a dynamism which has no longer any assignable finite goal.

There is ultimately only one name for that endlessly distant reality which such love silently evokes—God. He is the guarantor of eternal love. He is the guardian of the dignity of the person who in love gives and entrusts himself to another fallible and limited human being. He is the fulfilment of the eternal promise which love implies but which it could not itself fulfil if it had itself to provide such ultimate fulfilment. He is the unfathomable depth (in grace) of the other human being without which in the long run every human being would become tedious and empty in the other's eyes. He is the endless expanse in which we find room to lighten the burdens which we do not want to impose on another, although they would crush us if we carried them alone. He stands as true forgiveness for both, behind and above every act of forgiveness without which no love in the long run can live. He is in person that sacred fidelity which we must love if we are to be able to be always faithful. In a word, he is the very love from which all other love derives and to which all other love must be open if it is not to be a venture which does not realize what it implies, and lead to disaster through its own infinity.

Only in its sacramental mystery, however, does God's hidden partnership in marriage come to full realization and become clearly known to us. From the message of faith we know that matrimony reaches up into the mystery of God in an even more radical sense than we can surmise even from the unconditional character of human love. Marriage is a sacrament, the Church tells us. We take that so much as a matter of course. But we have to understand what that means if we are to appreciate the almost strangely disturbing boldness with which the highest is affirmed of such an apparently commonplace human business. Marriage between Christians is a sacrament. It therefore confers grace. Grace, however, does not only mean God's help for married people to be loving and faithful, patient, sturdy, unselfish, bearing one another's burdens. Grace does not mean only God's help to fulfil tasks and duties which everyone recognizes as belonging to this world and, at least in theory, accepts. Grace means more. It means divine life, the strength of eternity, a participation, earnest, seal and anointing, beginning and ground of that life which, caught up into the life of God himself, is worthy of being lived a whole eternity. Grace ultimately means God himself who wishes to lavish himself without intermediary on his spiritual creature with the infinite plenitude of his life and inexpressible glory.

It is true that all this is still hidden under the veils of faith and hope, that it is all still incomprehensible and obscure; it may not yet have emerged from the deepest depths of our mind into the flatness of our dull everyday experience. But it all exists nevertheless, and by the slight, arid word "grace" we mean precisely all this, which God has effected in the innermost but to us still inaccessible centre of our being, as the seed of the life of eternity, of freedom final in its blessedness. We say that the sacrament of matrimony increases this grace which is not simply a daily divine help to morally right action. That means, therefore, that when Christians marry, when a sign of indissoluble love is established in this world, which is a symbol of Christ's redemptive love for his Church, grace occurs, i.e. divine life occurs. If it is not prevented by the mortal guilt of the lovers, a new dynamism begins which can carry them deeper into the life of God. New depths of divine glory are opened out in that region of the spirit in which God himself communicates himself to it as the life of the soul. There the love which unites man with his God grows to more delicate tenderness and stronger fidelity. There the one mystery of all human life occurs even more profoundly and vitally, more strongly and unconditionally than before: the finding of God in the immediate presence of his own communication to the inner man.

That is the really consumingly bold and divine thing that is affirmed when it is said that marriage is a sacrament. It is affirmed that marriage is not only a communion of love between two human beings but, while remaining such, is also a communion of grace with God himself. No doubt that does not occur without regard to man and his freedom or without his interior consent. There is no doubt, therefore, that the lovers only experience this reality in proportion as they open their hearts to it in faith and love. But God wills this grace to occur and therefore this meeting with God himself in grace can and must occur even here and now.

Consequently marriage is really a mystery of God, a part of the liturgy in which the mysteries of eternity become present in a sacred rite which bestows salvation.

The liturgy of conjugal consent leads into the celebration of the holy sacrifice. That is as it should be. The grace of matrimony is the grace of Christ. Consequently it comes from the source of all grace, the pierced heart of the redeemer who, on the altar of the Cross, gave himself for the Church his bride, by allowing himself to fall into the boundless darkness of death, confident that in this way he was committing his soul into the hands of his Father by giving it with holy generosity for the salvation of all. All grace comes from the pierced heart of Christ, and so therefore does the grace of matrimony, without which no marriage can be good and blessed. Consequently, the grace of marriage too bears the stamp of its origin. It is the grace of sacrificial love, the grace of forgiving, enduring, excusing, unselfish love which hides its pain. It is the grace of a love which is true to death, fruitful for life and in death, the grace of that love which Paul praises, which is kind, which believes all things, bears all things, hopes all things, endures all things, which never ends, without which all else is nothing. When, therefore, in a sacred festival before the holy altar of God we link the celebration of such a marriage with the celebration of the highest act of Christ's sacrificial love for his Church, what we are doing is itself a prayer and opens men's hearts to such love.

"He who calls you is faithful, and he will do it", says Paul (1 Thess 5:24) regarding men's development as Christians. Now a sacrament is indeed a part of this Christian development. And so, trusting to the power of grace and of the divine promise, we can also apply this saying to the loving community of the married couple. To have received the sacrament of matrimony is to have been called by God to share God's own love by love for one's partner. And it is he himself who comes to the help of the weak and effects the divine accomplishment of human married love. Husband and wife must therefore give themselves to him, to the blessed power of his grace, which flows from the heart of the dying Lord, in order to give their conjugal devotion that depth and purity which its very nature calls for and demands.

SAINTS' DAYS

The Feast-Day of a Holy Beginning

The feast of Mary's Immaculate Conception

In the Kingdom of God, the kingdom of love, all is bestowed on each in his own particular way, the whole pervades and prevails in each, and each of the mysteries of the Kingdom is inexhaustible. It has only been grasped perfectly when all has been understood. The whole, however, is the inexhaustibility of the infinite mystery of God. Consequently the mystery of the feast of the Immaculate Conception can be regarded under innumerable aspects. No one is forbidden to seek the particular aspect which leads him best and most fully into this mystery of God, so that he comes to God himself.

We wish to consider this as the feast of beginnings. We shall reflect on the beginning as such, on the beginning of the blessed Virgin, and on our own.

I. The beginning as such. A beginning is not empty nothingness, something inconsiderable, hollow indeterminacy, what is inferior and general. That is the sort of way people mostly think today, and regard everything lofty and perfect (if they are still capable of conceiving and loving such things) as a complicated amalgam of the least precious, uniformly unremarkable, "basic elements". But the true beginning of what comes to high perfection is not empty vacuity. It is the closed bud, the rich ground of a process of becoming, which possesses what it can give rise to. It is not the first and smallest portion at the beginning of a process of becoming, but the whole of the history which is beginning, in its radical ground.

For the beginning as such is God, the plenitude of all reality. And when it is said of us that we are created from "nothing", that does indeed mean that we are not God, but it does not mean that our origin was the void, an indeterminacy indifferent to everything, it means it was God. And God posits the created beginning which is not the first moment of our time but the original ground of the whole history of our freedom in time. For that reason the beginning is posited solely by God; it is his mystery which inaccessibly rules over us. Consequently it only reveals itself slowly in the course of our history. That is why it has to be accepted by us in its darkness and obscurity, with trust, hope and courage. It has to be preserved by holy anamnesis in its inaccessible mystery and in what it discloses of itself in our history. For if that beginning is the permanent ground of human existence, and supports all, and is not something which we leave behind us as past and done with, then that beginning is the purpose of life, the content of the anamnesis which in a sacred rite renders the origin present. That is why we celebrate the birthday, the baptism and the Pasch of the Lord. These are all festivals of the beginning which is allotted to us as men and as Christians. And when we look forward with hope into the future, it is the manifestation of the beginning we are watching for. It is the beginning which is approaching us in the end, in the future the origin which has been acquired through history. If we fail to attain the fulfilment, it will be because we have lost the beginning. And if the end is pure fulfilment, then the beginning must have been a pure origin from infinite love. In the Gospel of Thomas we read "The disciples said to Jesus, 'Tell us what our end will be like'. Jesus said, 'Have you already discovered the beginning and yet you ask about the end? Blessed is he who will stand at the beginning and will know the end and not taste death'." The historical Jesus certainly did not make this statement. Yet if correctly read it is true nevertheless. Yet Jesus in reality did judge the present as a falling away from the pure beginning as this was posited by God and as it was to be re-established by himself, when he said, "In the beginning it was not so". And when Heidegger observes that origin always remains future, he expresses the same relation between beginning and fulfilment that the historical and the Gnostic Jesus affirm. We must first recall this general character of a beginning when we are celebrating the feast day of a pure beginning.

II. The Blessed Virgin's beginning. If we have understood what a beginning really means, we will understand that what the Church professes in regard to the Blessed Virgin's beginning is only the correct transposition into the beginning of what the Church always knew about the Blessed Virgin from her later life and from her significance in sacred history for the Church. This is so, however long it may have taken the Church to accomplish this regress from the consequence to the origin, from what was brought about to what was projected, from future to source, until the Church finally reached the definition of 1854. God as beginning and the beginning posited by God may not be separated in Mary through the difference established by the guilt of mankind. For this difference was not permitted prior to Christ and as superior to his redemptive work, but in subordination to it. He, as the absolute and unconditional will of God for his world even prior to the world and its sin, was the pure and primordial beginning of God's will for the finite. Guilt was only admitted because it remained enveloped within this hidden beginning which from the start was the overflowing spring of grace, even if its previously hidden plenitude was only manifested in the actual course of its flow. Mary, however, belongs to the will of the eternal God, the absolute will of God for the incarnation of his Logos which had already taken sin into account. Mary belongs to the beginning which contains, not to the beginning which is contained. She belongs to it of course as a posited, not as the positing beginning, as posited in God's will for the world, for the incarnation of the Logos and through this for redemption; therefore she belongs to it as a beginning redeemed in advance. And so she belongs to God's action within which he redemptively comprises sin, because in the concrete order this action of God in the incarnation of the Logos is inseparable from her in her flesh and her obedience. As a consequence there cannot be that difference in herself between the divinely established beginning of each human being as such and the beginning of the individual inasmuch as he remains conjoined to the guilty beginning of humanity as a whole, the deed of Adam. Her beginning is a pure, innocent and simple one, sheer grace, an element in the object of the redemption itself. God with absolute love always willed Mary as she who would say Yes to his own word addressed to the world. For this absolutely unconditionally willed word of grace is only spoken absolutely if it is heard obediently and in the flesh, precisely by Mary in fact. Because she was so willed, and because she was willed unconditionally, she was willed from and in the beginning as accepting. She cannot in the beginning be posited in her beginning as capable of saying No. She is endowed with grace in her beginning. Purely for the sake of Christ who is the redeemer, and therefore as an element in what is prior to the redemption, and for the sake of which God merely permitted guilt. This beginning is the disposition of God alone, the moment when God's love bestowing itself on man is still collected, concentrated in itself or rather, is originally immanent in itself as a love which has already forestalled guilt and which, because of this power, permits the weakness of guilt. Where this love posits such a created historical beginning, there is the beginning of the Blessed Virgin. Nevertheless, or rather, precisely in this way, this glory of a pure beginning originating in God was a beginning which had to be experienced with sorrow. The origin meant a future of everyday life, customary things, silence, the seven sorrows and the death of her Son and her own death. Only then was the beginning attained by the future retrieving the beginning. Only then was it disclosed as pure grace.

III. Our beginning. It is hidden in God. It is decided. Only when we have arrived will we fully know what our origin is. For God is mystery as such, and what he posited when he established us in our beginning is still the mystery of his free will hidden in his revealed word. But without evacuating the mystery, we can say that there belongs to our beginning the earth which God has created, the ancestors whose history God ruled with wisdom and mercy, Jesus Christ, the Church and baptism, earth and eternity. All is there, everything whatsoever which exists is silently concentrated in the well-spring of our own existence and all the rest is pervaded by what each in himself and therefore as a beginning posited by God uniquely and unrepeatedly is. With what is hard and what is easy, delicate and harsh, with what belongs to the abyss and what is heavenly. All is encompassed by God, his knowledge and his love. All has to be accepted. And we advance towards it all; we experience everything, one thing after another, until future and origin coincide. One thing about this beginning, however, has already been said to us by the word of God. The possibility of acceptance itself belongs to the might of the divinely posited beginning. And if we accept, we have accepted sheer love and happiness. For even if in our beginning the difference between God's will and human will is interposed, even if even in the beginning our lot is decided both by God *and* by the history of guilt, nevertheless precisely in our case even this contradiction is always merely permitted and is already encompassed by pure love and forgiveness. And the more that love and forgiveness which encompasses and belongs to our beginning is accepted in the pain of life and in the death which gives life, and the more this original element emerges and is allowed to manifest itself and pervade our history, the more the difference, the contradiction in the beginning is resolved and redeemed. And all the more will it be revealed that we ourselves were also implied in that pure beginning whose feast day we are celebrating. When the beginning has found itself in the fulfilment and has been fulfilled in the freedom of accepting love, *God* will be all in all. Because then all will belong to all, the differences will of course still be there but they will have been transformed and will belong to the blessedness of unifying love, and no longer to separation. And for that reason this feast is *our* feast. For it is the feast of the freely bestowed love in which all of us are comprised, each in his place and rank.

"Take the Child and his Mother"

On devotion to St Joseph

If this meditation turns out to be rather problematic, raising questions but giving rather uncertain answers, that need not matter. A good question is better than an answer which is only the semblance of one.

Why do we honour St Joseph?[1] An ordinary Christian will answer, because Joseph was a holy man and also the husband of the blessed Virgin and our Lord's foster-father. That is a good answer if correctly understood. But perhaps there is room for a certain doubt about it. Why? In the first place Joseph is praised in scripture as a just man (Mt 1:19), and even though this is only done in one particular context, it may rightly be regarded as a sort of bull of canonization. We assume without question, then, that he is a saint. But no one who knows how we honour Joseph and how devotion to him has developed since the end of the Middle Ages[2]

---

[1] Cf. in general from the literature on St Joseph: J. Müller, *Der heilige Joseph. Die dogmatischen Grundlagen seiner besonderen Verehrung* (1931); Henri Rondet, *Joseph von Nazareth, Gestalt und Verehrung* (1956).

[2] Cf. on this the account (with bibliography) given by J. Blinzler, „Joseph I/II" in: *Lexikon für Theologie und Kirche,* vol. V (2nd ed., 1960), cols. 1129–30.

down to his proclamation as protector of the universal Church will deny that this biblical canonization which itself would make of him a truly holy and just individual, is itself insufficient foundation for the position and honour which the Church in modern times has accorded him. But after all, it will be retorted, he is Jesus's foster-father and the husband of the Mother of God. Certainly he is, and scripture attests it. But is the scope and meaning of this testimony really plain and clear to us? To a certain extent this is open to doubt. The reason can be stated at once. Not every relation of kinship to Jesus, the Word of God who came into the flesh of sin, is in itself a reason for election of a kind which, while sanctifying the relative, draws him into the official, public history of the economy of redemption.

Position in official sacred history and inner holiness

This statement must be briefly explained before we can pursue our real question. The public history of redemption attested by God's word addressed to all is not present at every point where salvation is effected, where a human being finds God's grace in the free action of God and the human being. That history is in some respect a separate domain in the total history of mankind. For only a small part of this whole history is interpreted for us in its ultimate meaning by God's word even now (before the Last Judgment), declaring that here salvation and not perdition took place, that here God himself intervened by his action in the history of his world and was accepted in faith for salvation. In this official, public history of redemption which not only takes place but is revealed as such, the situation is actually as follows.[3] There is indissoluble unity, at least in the definitive sacred history of the New Testament, between the external event in sacred history and the inner sanctifying accomplishment of that history by the human beings who are called and who freely enact the divinely effected sacred history. Outside this official, public redemptive history proclaimed by God even now as the history of his victorious mercy, a human being can do something great and even important for God and his Kingdom and yet interiorly have failed, by refusing himself to God; office and holiness can diverge, fail to coincide. That cannot be the case in the actual public and official sacred history of the new and eternal, eschatological covenant of grace which is not merely proffered but victorious. Otherwise the visible sign which purports to be God's victorious presence would be inwardly void, a demonstration of something divine but remote, not an embodiment of the victorious grace which not merely offers itself to the world but overcomes its resistance and itself gives what it requires of us. The Church itself as a whole is not merely the proclamation of the law and the offer of grace, not only God's holy institution. It is a fulfilment of the law given as a gift, a victorious grace whose victory is visible and apparent, a really sanctified community of the redeemed. In fact it is precisely Church and not Synagogue. All the more so, then, is this true of that sacred history in the strictest and plainest sense, in which the salvation which remains present in the Church physically appeared. Here office and holiness, mission to others and personal endowment with grace, charis and charisma cannot be separated. Here what is announced in tangible history

[3] Cf. on what follows K. Rahner, *Theological Investigations,* vol. I (1959), vol. III (1967) and *Schriften zur Theologie,* vol. V (2nd ed. 1964), pp. 115–35.

must take place in the depth of reality. Here history, and therefore what is visible, is really redeemed, i.e., *is* the real presence of what it expresses, the efficacious "sacrament" of grace. Consequently, for example, the Church is we might almost say naively convinced that the apostles on whom the Spirit descended at the Pentecostal foundation of the Church and on whom he founded the visible Church, were also in fact men filled with God, endowed with grace and holiness, and that they remained so, so that on the twelve foundation stones of the new Jerusalem the names of the twelve apostles remain inscribed for all eternity (Rev 21:14). And for that reason the Church knows that Mary is not simply the mother of Jesus in the biological order, but *holy* Mary, the *blessed* virgin, holy in body and soul, redeemed, and the mother of grace, that in her, office corresponds to interior holiness and vice versa. Mission in the public history of redemption and interior sanctity perfectly correspond in her. This fundamental conviction is the basis of all the Church's knowledge about Mary.

Does Joseph also belong to this public history of redemption, so that the principle just referred to applies to him also? If this were not so, we should really know no more about Joseph than the brief remarks we find in scripture. These would have to be read not as statements about a redemptive reality but as biographical marginal notes such as are unavoidable in narrating redemptive history but do not really denote an object of that history. Joseph would of course be in close relation with Jesus, but as little would be deducible from this as there is regarding Jesus's other relatives who are mentioned as his "brothers" and "sisters", for we have no right to conclude that special holiness is to be attributed to them. The ancient Church expressly saw only one figure among those around Jesus whom it counted

among the positive agents of redemptive history, apart from
Mary and the apostles, and that was John the Baptist. And
for centuries he caused Joseph to be overlooked. More is
expressly reported of him in scripture. It is clearer that he
really belongs as an active figure in the official drama that is
enacted between God and humanity. As a result the liturgy
of the ancient Church honoured him much earlier than the
Lord's foster-father and in some respects honours him in a
more solemn way even to this day. Does this involve a matter
of principle and a limit, or has the Church gradually learnt
to see more clearly that Joseph too really belongs to the
history of redemption as such? In dealing with this we can
omit the question of how we can solve theologically the
apparent contradiction between the ancient and modern
liturgy of the Church in the fact that formerly it was John
who was the *felix patriarcharum clausula* whereas that title is
now applied to Joseph.

On the exegesis of Matthew 1

In order to answer this question or at least to attempt an
answer, a detailed exegesis of the first chapter of Matthew
would be needed. This cannot be done in a really satis-
factory way here, or in the present state of scholarship.
Researches using the methods of form-history (such as
A. Vögtle and others have already carried out for Matthew 2)
are indispensable. The following interpretation is on very
much simpler lines, for several reasons. The general
agreement of traditional Catholic exegesis of this passage
must be shown to be disputable on the basis of the text
itself. Even an exegesis using the most modern methods
must not forget simply to listen to the actual statements of

the text. A Catholic theologian in particular cannot forget this. And elaborate constructions are not required for it. Finally it remains quite legitimate even from the theological point of view for such an interpretation to bring more clearly to light a theological affirmation of scripture, even if this is not done solely by the methods of philological and genetic inquiry. This is not intended to anticipate the results of thorough exegetical work. The account we give is consciously provisional, but nevertheless remains closer to the text and the meaning of scripture itself, I think, than the usual interpretation. For similar reasons no detailed discussion of the relevant bibliography is undertaken.

Every Christian is familiar with the words of Matthew 1:

"Now the birth of Jesus Christ took place in this way. When his mother Mary had been betrothed to Joseph, before they came together she was found to be with child of the Holy Spirit; and her husband Joseph, being a just man and unwilling to put her to shame, resolved to send her away quietly. But as he considered this, behold, an angel of the Lord appeared to him in a dream, saying, 'Joseph, son of David, do not fear to take Mary your wife, for that which is conceived in her is of the Holy Spirit; she will bear a son, and you shall call his name Jesus . . .' When Joseph woke from sleep, he did as the angel of the Lord commanded him; he took his wife . . ."
(Mt 1:18–24)

The text is almost always understood by exegesis and pious reflection to mean that Joseph did in fact observe that Mary was pregnant but did not know how to account for this state of affairs; that he was informed about the miraculous conception neither by a question of his own nor by Mary's initiative. Because of this situation he wanted to send her away. An attempt is then made to elaborate a very sublime psychology to explain why Mary and Joseph were silent, why precisely Joseph decided to send Mary away, and why he intended to do this secretly.

Is this interpretation correct? In the first place the text clearly states that Mary was found to be with child of the Holy Spirit. No one doubts that the condition the discovery of which is noted here was observed by *Joseph*. But people arbitrarily correct the text: they say "of the Holy Spirit" is an addition which does not really belong here. It is said to be an explanation by the author of a fact which Joseph only learnt later, from the mouth of the angel. But that is not what stands in the text. Such weakening of what is said would only be justified if the narrative did not otherwise make sense. Let us assume that Joseph noticed Mary's condition, asked her about it and was informed of its heavenly origin. Then the statement has its full meaning: Mary was found (by Joseph) to be with child of the Holy Spirit. Why should that not have been what happened? In order to explain why it could not have happened like that, a very tortuous psychology is postulated: Joseph does not ask. But why exactly shouldn't he have asked Mary? What more natural than such a question, precisely in regard to a woman whom he trusted and loved? And why should Mary have been silent? Had she no trust in Joseph and his willingness to believe? If Mary was acting appropriately, calmly and clearly, could she rely on Joseph's hearing from some other source what after all he had to hear from her point of view, since for her part she did not intend to leave him? And if she did intend to stay with him, she would have to tell him the reason for her pregnancy now that he had noticed it. He had a right to this. And the wise Virgin could not reasonably count on Joseph's being informed miraculously of something which he could and must hear

about from herself. He at least had a right to that if Mary
intended to remain with him as her husband. Mary does not
give the impression in other matters that she was incapable
of carrying out normal everyday duties (even if they resulted
from very heavenly events) in a very ordinary and normal
way.

But according to the text Joseph learns from the *angel*
that Mary has conceived of the Holy Spirit? Certainly, but
does this have to be the *first* information he received about
the fact? Can this not be regarded as a heavenly confirmation
of what he had heard from Mary? Would a "second witness"
be superfluous and meaningless in such a question, which
demanded the uttermost effort of faith? By no means. Even
for this reason it is quite arbitrary to try to infer from verse
20 that Joseph could not previously have known anything
about the heavenly origin of the child. If then verse 18 (if
we leave it its full, straightforward sense) means that Joseph
already knew about it, this fact is not belied by verse 20.
Furthermore, this message of the angel about the child's
heavenly origin is not merely a confirmation of Joseph's
knowledge already acquired from Mary, but is introduced
as the reason for something else, as we shall see. There is a
justification for the angel's making the statement which is
independent of the question whether Joseph himself was
already aware of the state of affairs or not. For in a particular
explanatory context it is possible meaningfully to refer to a
fact which purely in itself is already known to the person
addressed.

But what of Joseph's intention to send Mary away quietly? Certainly. But this too is more intelligible if we assume
that he already knew of the supernatural origin of the child.

In the first place, if Joseph knew nothing about this, why
did he intend to send Mary away quietly? If he had suspected

an immoral cause of the pregnancy, what would be the motive for that intention and why would that intention be a sign of a special "justice" i.e. from the point of view of the Old Testament, a determination to fulfil the whole written Law? On such a hypothesis neither is intelligible. But if Joseph had no thought of such an adulterous cause, and on the other hand knew nothing of the supernatural cause of the conception, he could not have had any explanation at all in mind for the conception. Is he really supposed then by this secret dismissal simply to have evaded a vital problem, which he could have solved by a simple and obvious question to his betrothed wife? It is absurd in this connection to talk of Joseph having left and entrusted everything to God. One only rightly entrusts an enigma in life to God in passive resignation when one has done one's best to solve it. But Joseph would only have done this if he had tried to find the reason for the pregnancy by a simple very natural question to somebody who was in a position to know the reason, i.e., someone among those with whom Joseph was concerned (he wasn't counting on angels), in other words, Mary. We have every reason to suppose that he did in fact do so. At all events Joseph's intention to send Mary away quietly is not explained by Joseph's ignorance of the history of the child's conception. If he had not known about it, he would inevitably have acted differently.

In fact the affianced husband's knowledge of the supernatural character of the conception explains his intention. He knows that heaven has sent this maiden a child; he has found her with child of the Holy Spirit. What more obvious than to regard himself as not belonging to this sacred history? Because Joseph knew from Mary the great thing that God had done in her, would he not inevitably say to himself, Here I can no longer have any claim on my betrothed?

Here heaven has claimed this person, and I must withdraw
if I am to be a just man? And in order that this withdrawal,
this abandonment of the claims acquired by betrothal should
not injure Mary, he would of course have to send her away
secretly.[4]

Naturally we can ask whether such a decision would have
been in every respect best for Mary in the circumstances
and whether a secret dismissal would not in fact have in-
jured her. In estimating in this way the possible disadvan-
tages, we should also of course have to ask whether Joseph
thought of sending Mary away before the birth of the child;
whether after sending her away at once or later the child
would have been publicly regarded as adulterous or as ille-
gitimately conceived before the home-taking or regarded
as Joseph's child. Since all this is difficult to say, we must
avoid inferring on the basis of speculations regarding
Mary's position if she had been dismissed, that Joseph could
not have intended to send the mother and child away if he
had known of the heavenly event. At all events we can say
that even on the supposition that Joseph knew nothing of

---

[4] The statement that Joseph did not wish to put her to shame is not
intended to give a reason for sending her away, but for doing so "quietly". If Joseph had dismissed Mary publicly by an explicit announce-
ment, she would have come under suspicion of having herself given some
culpable ground for the dismissal, whatever those around her took this
to be. (They need not necessarily, of course, have sought this cause in the
pregnancy itself, for we cannot say for certain when Joseph had intended
to send Mary away nor whether the neighbours would not in any case
have regarded the child as Joseph's). Joseph could not in any case have
entertained the hope that the neighbours would believe in the child's
miraculous origin. A generally noticed dismissal would, therefore, in
any event have thrown suspicion on Mary. The statement that Joseph
did not wish to put Mary to shame does not therefore prove either
suspicion in Joseph's mind nor that he himself knew nothing of the
heavenly mystery before the angel's message.

the heavenly event, he did not intend to harm Mary by sending her away. The text sufficiently indicates this. The circumstances must therefore have been such that a wise and
thoughtful man did not have to fear particular harm for
mother and child. If this was so in any case, we cannot say
that Joseph would necessarily have had to take Mary and
the child to himself if he had known the mystery, as otherwise he would have harmed them, which on this hypothesis he did not wish to do.

We can therefore confidently say that Joseph knew the
heavenly origin of the event and of the child, and for that
very reason wanted to withdraw as being foreign to it and
not concerned in it. He did not wish to claim for himself
her whom God had claimed. Joseph therefore did not in
fact think as "Josephology" since Augustine's time[5] has considered him to have done: For my part I have paternal
rights over this child; I am his father because this child, even
though by the miracle of heaven, has come into existence
in my marriage, because the mother is my wife. Quite apart
from the question whether by the marriage laws of that
time it was possible in principle to regard in that way the
child of a woman who was simply betrothed but had not
yet been taken to her husband's home, Joseph did not think
in those terms about the relation between himself and the

[5] Cf. Augustine, *Sermo* 51 n. 17–21 (*PL* 38, 342–45); *Contra Julianum* V
n. 46 f. (*PL* 44, 810f.); *Sermo* 225 n. 2 (*PL* 38, 1096); *De consensu evang.* II,
23 (*PL* 34, 1071–72). By this criticism of this "masterpiece of the theology of marriage" (as Rondet calls it, *op. cit.,* p. 110), and which Müller
too praises (*op. cit.,* p. 116), we do not wish to deny that once the natural
bond between Mary and Joseph was raised as it were from on high into
the sphere of the history of salvation and grace, and in a certain sense
had become sacramental, all that Augustine says is perfectly correct. On
this doctrine of Augustine, cf. especially Müller, pp. 108–20.

child of heaven and its mother. He did not take this saving event as something which had to fit into the framework of his earthly circumstances, which were what were properly his, but as something which cancelled his earthly rights, as far as they were really his, so that from the fact of his earthly betrothal he no longer had, and therefore did not make, any further claims on the mother and child.

Joseph the officially appointed father of Jesus

We have reached the point for the sake of which this whole exegetical inquiry was undertaken. By the appearance of the angel Joseph is appointed to be what he was not on the lower plane, by the mere fact of his betrothal: the husband of *this* virgin, the father of *this* child. He is incorporated into the history of redemption as such. The saviour of the world is really entrusted to him from above for us. And therefore Jesus is heir to the promise made to David because he is the son of Joseph the son of David, as the angel expressly calls him. That is why the angel does not encourage him to do what was his hereditary right, but commands him to do what he otherwise could not really do: take his wife to himself. That is why it is expressly said that he did this in obedience to the angel's command. That is why he took "the child and his mother" (Mt 2:13, 14, 21), a phrase that occurs three times. Joseph therefore does not stand only in a private and purely natural relationship to Jesus, like his "brothers" and "sisters" for example, who cannot be declared blessed on that account; far from it. Their relationship to Jesus, though closer by blood than Joseph's conferred on them no rights in the Kingdom of God and no holiness. Joseph does not stand at the end of Jesus' genealogical tree (Mt 1:16; Lk 3:23) as one of the sinners of whose race the redeemer willed to assume the sinful flesh (Rom 8:3). He stands in redemptive history as a man who has been taken into the beginning of that new line of life which is no longer born of the will of the flesh. He is the guardian and protector of the Son who is from above, and he is so by a heavenly commission which he accepts obediently in faith. He too is declared blessed (though in different terms) because his natural relationship to Jesus has been raised and incorporated into his supernatural act of faith, precisely as with Mary (cf. Lk 1:45 with Lk 11:27 f.). It is not simply as if what is earthly were excluded unsaved from the action of the grace-giving Holy Spirit (for all flesh is to see the salvation of God), but neither is it the case that blood relationship to Jesus in its own right and without change, entered into the heavenly events of charisma and charis, office and endowment with grace. The ancestors of Christ (Rom 9:5) "according to the flesh", like all others, have first to become through the "Spirit" those of whom the Lord can say that they are his brother, sister and mother (Mt 12:50). But what scripture attests for us is precisely that Joseph is decisively more than a blood relative of Jesus according to the flesh, belonging to his private biography but not really to the anamnesis of the history of the Kingdom of God. For scripture shows us Joseph becoming Jesus' father through heavenly intervention at the moment when by his own intention he professes that he is not his earthly father. When we read in scripture that we are built up on the foundation of the apostles and prophets, when it is said, therefore, that our eternal salvation and destiny rests for ever on their obedience in faith as it does on that of Abraham, then St Joseph too belongs in this list of the fathers of our salvation. And he does so at the place where he stands, beside the child who is salvation itself. While Joseph regards the child's conception through the Holy Spirit as a reason which makes it a duty in justice for him to withdraw, the angel declares this fact to be precisely the reason for his duty to stay. This holy one must be protected, he must be surrounded by the conjugal love and community of Mary and Joseph, he must be a holy one who is *accepted,* at least by a holy remnant, even if his own in general do not receive him (Jn 1:11).

This is where we must seek the starting-point for an understanding of Joseph's office and holiness which we spoke of at the beginning of our reflections. Only in the light of what has been said is it clear what is meant by saying that Joseph is the husband of the Mother of God and Jesus's foster-father and *therefore* St Joseph as the Church's devotion knows him. He indubitably has a holiness which corresponds to his function in public sacred history. For at the point where salvation took place for all time, he was called from above into the actual public history of redemption, with an office which actually contributed to it. We should not really know his holiness otherwise. We could only hope and assume that he obtained salvation, but we should know this as little as we know it regarding any of the nameless ancestors and relatives of the Lord. He belongs to sacred history in such a way that this became salvation in him and for him. He truly belonged to it at least as the apostles and John the Baptist did. On this basis the attempt can be made to explain the thesis of a protodulia (prime homage) paid to St Joseph, which has been defended in theology for a long time; then it may not seem a strangely excogitated little invention of idle speculation. For the Imitation of Christ and Ignatius Loyola warn us not to wish to determine too precisely the rank of God's saints in his Kingdom.

We too are often called to be guardians of something holy which is to be born in the world and from its mysterious bosom. To be its guardians in ourselves, in our life, profession and work. To all appearance only everyday things are involved which have nothing to do with the sacred history of the Kingdom of God and the salvation of the world. And in fact, we and our actions do not belong to the public history of redemption which has already been revealed by God even now while time is still unfolding and we are still pilgrims in faith. It is not yet manifest that we are children of God. We hope we are, and run, without calculating and looking back, with fear and trembling and with firm hope, towards what God's grace may have given us to be. But even if not manifestly and openly, our life must and can in a hidden way be sacred history, history of the Kingdom of God and of the victory of grace, birth of Christ in the flesh, preservation and defence of what is holy, as in Joseph's story. To all appearances it is only for our own happiness and by our own decision that we form ties and relationships in life, bonds of acquaintance, love and business. Fundamentally, however, in these we are people called and endowed with grace, the guardians of what is holy in faith, courage, fidelity and obedience, like Joseph. Earthly love becomes a sacrament and marriage the origin of an eternal destiny full of the glory of grace. And who does not have children of God entrusted to them, who are to continue the life of *the* child of God as such in time? They are entrusted to us in the family, as neighbours, at work, in school, children of God great and small who, of course, before God and in their concern for eternal life, all remain children — weak, poor and in need of help, dependent on faithful care. No angel from heaven appears to us to explain this heavenly task and to say to us: "Take this child of eternity which you

could not and would not be permitted to care for if you were
not commanded to from above. Take the child because it *is*
committed to you." And yet to us, too, through the equally
heavenly message of faith, of the Gospel, the same charge
has been allotted, even though it has not been revealed to
us by the same voice, that we have also actually accepted it.
Only through apparently earthly events and circumstances
is what is heavenly and divine, God's grace, its continuance
and victory in our own hearts and our earthly surroundings
entrusted to us. Everywhere the Son of God who became
man continues to live his life. Everywhere we are asked
whether we shall be found as faithful in guarding this child
who meets us in all his brothers and sisters (and even in ourselves) as Joseph was, of whom it is written: He was a just
man. He took the child and its mother, protected them a-
broad and at home in good times and in bad. He guarded
the child so that it could become what it was, the saviour of
the world.

Thomas Aquinas

I

When we are celebrating the feast of St Thomas and, as is right and proper, are thinking about the patron of theological studies, and ponder on him in our meditation, perhaps the first thing we might consider for a moment is Catholic veneration of saints in general. It is a specifically Catholic thing within Western Christianity, and rightly so. But we must understand what this honour paid to saints really means. Then we shall realize that on this point we are not at all as Catholic nowadays as we perhaps think we are. Veneration of the saints is not merely historical remembrance of a past which is important from a human and ecclesiastical point of view. It is a real and genuine relation to a living person who has attained perfect fulfilment and therefore remains present and powerful. Veneration of the saints is faith, hope and love; it means being drawn into the Kingdom of God in its perfect fulfilment which has already dawned. And this is where probably all or at least most of us have difficulties. That does not attract us at all for our part today. Religion for us has become concentrated in a very remarkable way on God. The absolute mystery is unique, and religion for us has come to mean appearing before that abyss of radical infinity and incomprehensibility. For us the dead are very dead and remote. The world of men has become fragile, strange, finite and above all secular. As a result, the saints have evaporated as it were into past history, into what is dead and gone. And although we do not deny their permanent existence, they have been swallowed up as it were and have disappeared under the one word which still expresses our present day religious feelings, God. Now this is not Catholic at all. And the old-fashioned, traditional Catholic practice of venerating the saints is something which still stands ahead of us almost like the distant goal of our own religious development, as a higher future. It means real, genuine, living realization of the fact that they exist, that they are living and powerful, that they are nearer to us than ever, that they are not absorbed by God but are confirmed by him, that he is truly the God of the living and not of the dead, that far from being destroyed if we approach him, it is only then that we attain our own plenitude and independence, for the real God does not need to reduce us to nothing. Veneration of the saints is not a sort of veiled polytheism nor a puerile kind of piety which has not yet properly realized the overwhelming power and awe-inspiring mystery of God. It is the maturity of the Christian relation to God. For that maturity is aware that the creature does not disappear in the abyss of God when it abandons itself to him, but only then becomes truly living and established. It can find the creature in God because that creature has entered into him but has not been swallowed up in him. And to find the creature in *God,* in *his* perfection, in God's definitive *self*-communication to this creature, is a genuine religious act which belongs to the maturity of man's relation to God. And the feature of that creature which is found in this way in God, the feature which is honoured and acknowledged as eternally valid, and lovingly embraced,

is not an imaginary continued existence and activity inter-
posing this perfected creature as a daimonion and intermediary entity between God and us. It is precisely the eternity
of that creature's earthly time, the irrevocable validity of
the life which it lived here. In regard to Jesus, the anamnesis
by which we turn back to his history as it was, and the in-
vocation of the exalted Lord, are two elements of one and
the same action. For if he had not been raised on high, his
history would have disappeared into the oblivion of the
past, and if he were not the historical figure who precisely
as such has become definitive and possesses his unique life
as his eternity, he could only be invoked on high as an idea
or an empty name or as an incalculable, unknown power.
So it is with the saints. Those whom we know from their
history we invoke as transfigured, because their history is
their fulfilment.

II

We shall mention a few facets of St Thomas' rich spiritual
personality which we know can be a blessed presence for us
even now if we open ourselves to them by honouring them.
We are well aware that the selection is arbitrary. Everyone
is free to interpret the picture of the saint from another
angle. But this being understood, we will say in the first
place that Thomas is sober and objective. Anyone who has
dipped into the Summa realizes this at once. His tone is
quiet, reserved, almost dull; he is at no pains to find im-
pressive words. He does not think it necessary to amplify
the great topic he is writing about with high-sounding
language, for that is quite impossible. He shows almost no
preference for certain themes of theology rather than others.
The whole is important to him and therefore every detail.

As a further consequence, he is not dazzled by detail; he always thinks on the basis of the whole and in relation to the whole. And because he does not seek to impress but is himself impressed by the reality he is talking about, because he himself is still meditating and assimilating that reality when he is attempting to convey it in words to others, it is almost as though he were speaking to himself, quietly, economically, patient with himself and the reality, courteous to his opponents, as far as he has any or could have, because of the inner breadth and capaciousness of his mind. He is a systematic thinker who always considers the individual in the light of clearly grasped first principles. But because he is objective, the individual never becomes a mere occasion for declaiming about principles. It is really and lovingly taken into consideration, even if at first sight it does not seem to fit into the great guiding themes of his thought. This objective sobriety and objectivity reveals or hides awe, reverence, a deeply moving virile modesty, longing for that eternal light which is still directly shining even now, and the awareness that even in theology knowledge is only really theological to the extent that it remains fully and permanently conscious of its own provisional and inadequate character. Thomas is objective and sober in his thought.

Thomas' theology is his spiritual life and his spiritual life is his theology. With him we do not yet find the horrible difference which is often to be observed in later theology, between theology and spiritual life. He thinks theology because he needs it in his spiritual life as its most essential condition, and he thinks theology in such a way that it can become really important for life in the concrete. In his spiritual life (we may recall his Eucharistic hymns) he never reverts to the elementary, as though he had never engaged in theology. He does not believe that the spiritual life

necessarily best develops on the basis of simplicity in the
sense of mental laziness and spiritual mediocrity. It would
be unthinkable for him, the theological scholar, to nourish
his spiritual life like some worthy monk, for example, on
the third-rate fare of the pious fantasies of some nun or
other who, no doubt in good faith, presented these vagaries
as divine revelations. And though we unfortunately for the
most part only study his Summa, we should not forget that
he himself regarded himself primarily as an interpreter of
holy scripture and that that function was simultaneously a
learned and a spiritual office for himself and others. He
speaks and composes hymns which combine depth, seriousness and simplicity and they are at once his theology and his
spiritual life. Because textbooks nowadays are very often
too unspiritual and spiritual books too untheological, there
is always too great a danger of theology becoming a disagree-
able hurdle which has to be overcome on the way to the
priesthood, and that later our spiritual life and preaching
draw on the small derivative rivulets of second-hand pious
literature and not from scripture and the lofty theology of
the Fathers and the great theologians. In Thomas, however,
theology and spiritual life are still one.

Thomas is the mystic who adores the mystery which is
beyond all possibility of expression. Thomas is not of the
opinion that because theology deals with the infinite mystery of God it may talk imprecisely and vaguely. But he is
not of the opinion either that the precise language of theology should give the impression that we have discovered the
secret and caught the mystery of God in the subtle nets of
theological concepts. Thomas knows that the highest
precision and sober objectivity of true theology ultimately
serve only one purpose: to force man out of the lucid clarity
of his existence into the mystery of God, where he no longer

grasps but is moved, where he no longer reasons but
adores, where he does not master but is overpowered. Only
where the theology of concepts and comprehension raises
itself and is transformed into the theology of overwhelming
incomprehensibility is it really theology. Otherwise it is at
bottom merely human chatter, however correct it may be.
The "Adoro te devote, *latens* Deitas, quae sub his figuris
vere latitas" must not always be recited lyrically; it must be
the central principle of all theological thought and knowledge. This is so not only now but in eternity. Even there,
where we know as we are known and see face to face, what
is seen, loved and praised will be the eternal mystery. It
gives itself to the heart as mystery and does not become
smaller thereby but even more incomprehensible and more
consuming than when it only manifests itself in signs and
likenesses. It cannot therefore be otherwise in the "theologia
viatorum". This must become instruction in the experience
of mystery as such, a mystery which has, of course, become
closely present. The idle, the mindless and heartless, the
lovers of comfort, must not say that all that theology has
to say is but straw, as Thomas said it was. But if a man of
mind and heart, industry and energy, has not like Thomas
become aware, even in theology, of the deadly yet vivifying
sadness, that all theology has to say is but "paleae", then he
hasn't done theology after the model of Thomas; it has
been clever but not pneumatic, not a genuine Thomism.

Thomas is alive. He is living *his* life with God. In God it
has become wholly pure and established in its utter purity.
It has remained his own and yet open into God's infinity
and into the incalculable range of other vocations. And
therefore each can say with genuine faith: St Thomas, pray
for me.

MYSTERIES OF THE APPARENTLY INSIGNIFICANT

An Ordinary Song

A lot of people nowadays hear a lot of music. One can get it from a wireless set like water from the tap; you only need to switch on. Very few people make music for themselves. Few sing, and even fewer can sing themselves a new song spontaneously. And yet presumably songs of that kind, like playing and dancing, are difficult to do without if we are to be human. A new song of that kind, someone's own, bringing a human being into conscious identity with himself, need not be great music. As well as the works of great minds in literature, painting, philosophy and theology, there are the wise, kind and sincere words of everyday life. Everyone can express himself in these and so come to know himself, and God himself does not forget them. As well as great music then, there are the ordinary songs.

They are just as important, because in them the ordinary man expresses himself, and he too has an eternal life in front of him and therefore is infinitely great. There have to be these ordinary songs which, once they hear them, people hum or quietly whistle to themselves in everyday life as their own, as if they rang like an echo of their own hearts through mind and sense. They help people to express their own nature to themselves in all its facets and depths and also to express it to the mystery of their existence, which we call God. And so they do not suffocate in silence for lack of expression. There also have to be songs of that kind where man is most man and aware of himself: where God meets him and he God. That is why even the ancient Church songs in the hymn books do not replace the songs that flow spontaneously from the heart. Those Church hymns are the necessary "tradition" of man singing in the presence of God. He must proclaim even in song that he has spiritual ancestors who have transmitted to him the eternal youth of God. But people also have to sing themselves, express the new and ever unique human being which each one in his own way is. What a deadly danger is revealed then, by the fact that nowadays only serious original religious music is created (or music that aims at being such). It is so solemn and official that it can be sung even in Church in full congregation at high mass and—is it not almost a dreadful irony?–is *only* sung there. Is it not alarming that there are very few new religious compositions which anyone can feel to be the music of his own private piety (by which he has to work out his eternal salvation in everyday life)? But oughtn't such music to exist? It ought to be possible to whistle it. It need not have any greater depth of meaning or feeling than everyday life can have. That is quite sufficient. It still contains plenty. Or does religion only belong to the sublime hours of life? Or did the Word who was made flesh not have the courage to endure the narrow limits of our routine? A new song of the ordinary kind we are talking about would come to people's lips when they were setting off thankfully in good humour for their holidays. Who thinks nowadays of humming to himself "All praise be to God" at such a moment? We just don't sing like that now, although let us hope we have the same things in mind. We ought to be able to give spontaneous expression to our sadness in a song and find relief. But who sings "O Sacred Head, surrounded" nowadays as they do the washing up? The rhythm of a long distance lorry might inspire a new religious song one day. Why not? Or does genuine religion only belong to Sunday feelings and to the higher consumer goods of civilization, for which the State must pay because otherwise it would cost too much?

One must have thought about these and suchlike things if one hears the French Jesuit Aimé Duval, in case one does not feel sure one can listen and join in straight away without embarrassment, cheerfully, humbly and artlessly. It is very easy to run something down out of hand as sentimental, spoiling it for oneself and others. But one ought not to be frightened of feeling. Only people with little intelligence will do that. The others can quietly have the courage to be "sentimental", that is, to trust to the spontaneous emotion of their heart.

Seeing and Hearing

Seeing and hearing are clearly the fundamental modes of human experience. To be able to say this we do not need to raise the old question of how many senses man actually possesses. Touch can perhaps be understood as a rudimentary form of seeing and it is clearly only in the domain of seeing and hearing that it becomes human experience, i.e., that it presents another person or another thing as objectively perceived. And what eater and smoker has not noticed that taste in the darkness is not fully itself? But even those who doubt this may take what we are going to say as meaning that hearing and seeing can be regarded as the particularly clear and exemplary kinds of spontaneous human experience generally. They need not therefore reject what follows as mistaken from the start.

Now a banal commonsense "philosophy" will regard hearing and seeing simply as two gates through which our human world and our environment enter into the domain of our subjectivity, as two bridges by which we cross the gap between "subject" and "object". Such everyday philosophy (that of Greco-Roman and Western provenance at any rate) will simply accept those two gates and bridges as factual data, with the subconscious feeling that "in themselves" they could be quite different from what they are and would then convey quite different experiences. It will point out that other biological organisms clearly have quite a different sensory world, that because of our particular senses very much escapes us which in itself is just as directly present around us, that the actual senses we possess are a very arbitrary a priori filter (though biologically useful) which selects a priori, shuts out much, opens no access to many things. We do not see infra-red, we do not hear the acoustic waves which a bat uses with its "radar", we have no direct receptive organ for radio waves etc. Consequently we only approach a wider range of material reality with the help of interposed apparatus. In short, we regard our powers of hearing and seeing more or less as an old wireless set which is unfortunately incapable of receiving short waves. Then at most we console ourselves for this primitive quality of our receptive mechanisms by saying that they are sufficient after all for the immediate indispensable purposes of life and in *that* respect are not badly constructed.

Clearly, however, this "commonsense philosophy" of seeing and hearing is too primitive. In the first place a genuine metaphysics of man cannot (though we cannot indicate the reasons for this here) regard our sense organs on the model of a microscope which is added to our will to see and which allows as much to be seen as its structure permits, this structure being independent of the person seeing. We do not merely *have* sense organs, we *are* sensibility. Our corporeality and therefore our sensibility is built from within, from the personal-intellectual subject himself. It is the permanent mode in which mind (i.e., the free subject open from the start to the totality of all possible reality) has of itself entered into the world. It cannot therefore be the case at all (if this view, which can only be indicated here, is correct) that the apparatus for hearing and seeing represented by our sense organs was fitted on to us from outside and could just as well be different. Their biological adaptation to their purpose is only intelligible as an expression of the fact that they are appropriate to us precisely as intellectual, personal beings who stand in real relation to the world generally, not just to our particular environment. (The dog as a nasal animal is, of course, from the biological point of view just as adapted by his sensibility to his life. So the question could be raised, for what purpose we have furnished ourselves with our apparatus precisely in this way.) We must therefore say, however bold the thesis may be, that if a receptive spiritual nature as such (not ours, which is already retro-determined by its sensibility) "proceeds" and consti- tutes its "receptive apparatus" on the basis of its own purposefulness, it will hear and see just as we do. Seeing and hearing are precisely the ways in which the mind opening itself to the whole of reality as such admits this reality in direct encounter. (And this meeting which one goes out to and admits—by hearing and seeing—is ultimate- ly meant as loving communication of corporeal spiritual persons in such a way that in it the promise of the absolute mystery of God is found. Seeing and hearing on the one hand and intercommunication on the other imply in their unity and difference the problem of the relation between the aesthetic and the moral and religious, which cannot of course be gone into here.) Naturally it is impossible here to give grounds for this thesis of the origin of sensibility in mind itself, which thereby shows itself to be sensitive by its very nature. This may be considered laughable, and as a warning it may be pointed out that someday on a distant star intelligent corporeal beings may be discovered who communicate with their environment by senses quite

different from sight and hearing. It may be objected, too,
that the present state of our scientific knowledge of the
world proves that on the one hand the human mind aims
at the whole of the world's reality but that hearing and
seeing directly offer only a tiny section of that reality. On
this basis the mind has to find its way indirectly into the
totality. Consequently, as a corporeal mind it could certainly be conceived as having wider gates to the world
from the start. Nevertheless let this thesis stand, and the
question raised what it involves if it is properly understood.
In the first place it is not ultimately the case that hearing
and seeing only furnish slight initial material which is
elaborated by the scientific mind until this achieves its own
self-constructed world of knowledge. On this view only
the latter is the mind's own, and at the same time nearest to
the real world "in itself", as a conscious image of the
objective world. And so the sensory material would only be
a strange and ultimately amorphous intermediary between
the objective world and the world of the mind. Because the
mind makes the sensibility proceed from itself as its own
faculty (as Aquinas says) and retains it within itself (anima
est forma corporis), the mind itself is perfectly in act when,
in accordance with its nature as mind (i.e., on its own basis
with its limitless horizon and with all that it is), it actually
hears and sees, accomplishes that "turning" (one might almost use the term "conversion") to the image, without
which there is no true knowledge, as Thomas knew, in his
doctrine of the "conversio ad phantasma", and Kant also,
for whom a concept without a perception remains empty.
The concrete form in its "light", given to it through the
medium of colours, the articulate word with the intelligible
perspective it implies, both with the infinity in which they
stand, bring fully into act the mind itself.

What is also given by or in addition to this visible and
audible form, is of two kinds, which must not be confused.
An amalgam of the two must not falsely take on the appearance of being what the mind in truth is seeking. First there
is the clear horizon of the mind's limitless range; only in this
is the concrete form what it is, standing out in relief but
causing that horizon to be experienced when the form is
seen or heard: the infinity of the enveloping mystery of holy
silence. When we have forms heard or seen whose source is
there, which lose themselves in that, cause that invisible and
unutterable to be experienced, we have "primordial forms"
(of nature or art) as, for example, the Apollo which Rilke
contemplates in his poem, or "primordial words". "Behind" these primordial forms there is nothing, for with
them everything is present, the infinite mystery which in
them is *there*. "How did St Benedict see the world in a
coal?—In all things everything is hidden and concealed",
we read in Angelus Silesius (*Cherubinischer Wandersmann*
IV, 159). Only if we see or hear in this way can we really see
and hear. That we for the most part do not see and hear like
that, but in a technical and utilitarian way see things as
possible objects of active manipulation in the service of our
biological self-affirmation whether everyday or scientific,
is no argument against it, but only against us in our inau-
thenticity and mediocre anonymity. We have laboriously to
re-learn such hearing and seeing today. What is called
"composition of place" in religious meditation has its basis
here. Similarly the doctrine of the "spiritual senses" in a
long Christian tradition and the practice of the "application
of the senses" in mystical contemplation in Ignatius Loyola.
And a Christian would have to reflect here on what the First
Letter of John says, "What we have heard, what we have
seen with our eyes, what we have looked upon and touched

with our hands, concerning the word of life . . . ". He would have to realize that the meaning of the incarnation of God's Logos and the fundamental experience evoked here by John would be destroyed if we were to suppose that seeing and hearing are merely the spring-board which we leave behind in order to attain true knowledge of an abstract, non-sensory and wordless kind.

Secondly there is abstract, conceptual science. No one must despise it. It belongs to man, he must dare to undertake it, not only for his biological self-affirmation but because he is a mind in the world. It also belongs to the practical activity by which, not content with a purely contemplative relation to the world, he must fulfil himself. But where philological and historical learning, all that belongs to the moral sciences of man, does not return to sight and hearing of concrete forms, they become empty talk. Where philosophy and theology are no longer in possession of fundamental words, they cease to be true philosophy and theology, language which subjects us to mystery. And the natural sciences? They have certainly enormously extended knowledge and power over things. But if their mathematically formulated statements about functional relationships in the physical world are not to become pure mathematics and webs of formal logic, they cannot lose the connection of reference to what is directly given in sense experience. What they mean physically and not merely mathematically can always ultimately only be made intelligible on the model of objects of direct sight and hearing. They imply an intention to exercise power, directed ultimately at what we corporeally experience. This widening of the biological vital space and theoretical knowledge of a scientific kind ultimately stands at the service of that mind which becomes open to absolute mystery in simple spontaneous sight and hearing of the world around it or in loving interpersonal relationships. And so all sciences lead back to that fundamental seeing and hearing of the primordial forms through which the holy and enveloping mystery becomes known to man—especially when the primordial form is man himself, the human face, the ever unique word of his love.

Is there not a conflict between seeing and hearing? Almost the whole Greek and Western tradition of philosophy has surely regarded man as contemplating the "phenomenon" of being, whereas Christian tradition from the Old Testament down to Luther's assertion that the ears alone are the organ of the Christian man, has surely understood the word addressed to us with power, which brings what it utters, "passive" hearing as opposed to "active" gazing, to be the fundamental mode of authentic human existence? Isn't the complaint made that people nowadays will not read (i.e., hear) any more, but only want to look at pictures? It would be a foolish undertaking to attempt to settle the dispute between eyes and ears and decide which of them derives more directly and more radically from the one source of authentic human life. Those who read in the Bible the saying of Jesus that the ears and eyes of his disciples were blessed (Mt 13:16) will perhaps not seek to settle the dispute at all because it is not a genuine one. For both are ways of possessing the world and both are modes of personal relationship and derive from the same ground. *Together* they form a single contact with the world and the one domain of the presence of the sacred mystery. We might simply say with Angelus Silesius (*Cherubinischer Wandersmann* V, 351): "The senses are in the spirit all one sense and act;—He who sees God tastes, feels, smells and hears him too."

But is it true that people today are changing from a humanity of the ear and the word into one of eye and sight?

Of course it is quite conceivable for there to be epoch-making changes in the way the ultimate confronts man (as for example men of the Old Testament had a book of God but were not allowed to make any image of God). But the change in question which is so much lamented at the present time might be explained much more simply, to the extent that it really exists. One might say that through modern sciences in their almost limitless differentiation, through the enormous number of books, through the unimaginable character of the statements of modern natural sciences, through the "demythologizing" of theology (which always also involves the removal of pictures and images from it, however fatefully necessary this process may be), the amount of talk (and vocabulary) in contrast to earlier times, has increased so monstrously in comparison with what is visible, that the appetite for the pictorial is now at bottom merely a legitimate attempt to preserve a balance between seeing and hearing. That empty talk is, as a consequence, parallelled by an equally futile and insatiable appetite for things to look at, is deplorable and threatening but not surprising. But man is "born to see and appointed to gaze". He can and must always re-learn how to see. With the concentrated gaze which makes forms blossom out before him, in their purity and as they emerge from their roots in mystery. They may be forms in perfect simplicity and beauty, or forms which (like the Crucified) inescapably represent what is incomprehensible from the dark depth of our destiny, forms which God has shaped or which we have composed for him. And because seeing is really man's act (more than the passivity of hearing) man himself is manifested in seeing, steps before us, reveals himself in the way he sees and what he makes to be the object of his gaze. According to scripture, in man's eyes we read his fear, his nostalgia, his pride, compassion, kindness, wickedness, ill-will, scorn, envy and falsity. We make ourselves by seeing and form ourselves by gazing. But we have to learn how to see. It is not only the "effort of understanding" (Hegel) that is demanded of man, but also the effort of "contemplation", because man has been given the grace of sight. The sublimest of discourse is the last moment before silence falls, the silence which expresses the ultimate. Man perhaps most easily learns to be silent when he is gazing. We Christians long for the "vision of God", and confess Christ to be the image of God (2 Cor 4:4) as well as his Word; it is therefore an important task and a holy, human and Christian art to learn to see. We only think we have always been able to, and that nothing is easier. May we say, adapting a saying of scripture, He who has eyes to see, let him see? May we say that only those who have learnt to see (with the eyes of love) will be blessed? Those who have learnt to see with an eye which is "sound" (Mt 6:22) have the true "view of the world".

PRAYER FOR HOPE

We ask you, God of grace and eternal life, to increase and strengthen hope in us. Give us this virtue of the strong, this power of the confident, this courage of the unshakable. Make us always have a longing for you, the infinite plenitude of being. Make us always build on you and your fidelity, always hold fast without despondency to your might. Make us to be of this mind and produce this attitude in us by your Holy Spirit. Then, our Lord and God, we shall have the virtue of hope. Then we can courageously set about the task of our life again and again. Then we shall be animated by the joyful confidence that we are not working in vain. Then we shall do our work in the knowledge that in us and through us and, where our powers fail, without us, you the almighty according to your good pleasure are working to your honour and our salvation. Strengthen your hope in us.

The hope of eternity, however, eternal God, is your only-begotten Son. He possesses your infinite nature from eternity to eternity, because you have communicated it to him and ever communicate it, in eternal generation. He therefore possesses all that we hope and desire. He is wisdom and power, beauty and goodness, life and glory, he is all in all. And he, this Son to whom you have given all, has become ours. He became man. Your eternal Word, God of glory, became man, became like one of us, humbled himself and took human form, a human body, a human soul, a human life, a human lot even in its most terrible possibilities. Your Son, heavenly Father, truly became man. We kneel in adoration. For who can measure this incomprehensible love of yours? You have loved the world so much that men take offence at your love and call the affirmation of the incarnation of your Son folly and madness. But we believe in the incomprehensibility, the overwhelming audacity of your love. And because we believe, we can exult in blessed hope: Christ in us is the hope of glory. For if you give us your Son, what can there be you have held back, what can there be which you have refused us? If we possess your Son to whom you have given everything, your own substance, what could still be lacking to us? And he is truly ours. For he is the Son of Mary, who is our sister in Adam, he is a child of Adam's family, of the same race as we are, one in substance and origin with man. And if we human beings in your plans and according to your will as creator are all to form a great community of descent and destiny, and if your Son is to belong to this one great community, then we, precisely we poor children of Eve, share the race and lot of your own Son. We are brothers of the only-begotten, the brethren of your Son, co-heirs of his glory. We share in his grace, in his Spirit, in his life, in his destiny through Cross and glorification, in his eternal glory. It is no longer *we* who live our life but Christ our brother lives his life in us and through us. We are ready, Father of Jesus Christ and our Father, to share in the life of your Son. Dispose of our life, make it conformable to the life of your Son. He wills to continue his own life in us until the end of time, he wills to reveal in us and in our life the glory, the greatness, beauty and the blessed power of his life. What meets us in life is not chance, is not blind fate but is a part of the life of your Son. The joy we shall receive as Christ's joy, success as his success, pain as his pain, sorrow as his sorrow, work as his work, death as a sharing in his death.

In one respect we ask especially for your grace. Make us share in Jesus' prayer. He is the great worshipper of God in spirit and in truth, he is the mediator through whom alone our prayer can reach to the throne of grace. We wish to pray in him, united with his prayer. May he, with whom we are united in his Spirit, teach us to pray. May he teach us to pray as he himself prayed, to pray at all times and not to slacken, to pray perseveringly, confidently, humbly, in spirit and in truth, with true love of our neighbour without which no prayer is pleasing to you. May he teach us to pray for what he prayed: that your name may be hallowed, your will be done, your Kingdom come to us, for only if we first pray in that way for your honour will you also hear us if we pray for ourselves, our earthly well-being and earthly cares. Give us the spirit of prayer, of recollection, of union with God. Lord accept my poor heart. It is often so far from you. It is like a waste land without water, lost in the innumerable things and trifles that fill my everday life. Only you, Lord, can focus my heart on you, who are the centre of all hearts and the Lord of every soul. Only you can give the spirit of prayer, only your grace is capable of granting me to find you through the multiplicity of things and the distraction of mind of everyday routine, you the one thing necessary, the one thing in which my heart can rest. May your Spirit come to the help of my weakness, and when we do not know what we should ask, may he intercede for us with inexpressible sighs, and you who know men's hearts will hear what your Spirit interceding for us desires in us.

Finally, however, I ask you for the hardest and most difficult, for the grace to recognize the Cross of your Son in all the suffering of my life, to adore your holy and inscrutable will in it, to follow your Son on his way to the Cross as long as it may please you. Make me sensitive in what concerns your honour and not merely for my own well-being, and then I also will be able to carry many a cross as atonement for my sins. Do not let me be embittered by suffering but mature, patient, selfless, gentle and filled with longing for that land where there is no pain and for that day when you will wipe all tears from the eyes of those who have loved you and in sorrow have believed in your love and in darkness have believed in your light. Let my pain be a profession of my faith in your promises, a profession of my hope in your goodness and fidelity, a profession of my love, that I love you more than myself, that I love you for your own sake even without reward. May the Cross of my Lord be my model, my power, my consolation, the solution of all obscure questions, the light of every darkness. Grant that we may glory in the Cross of our Lord Jesus Christ, grant us to become so mature in true Christian being and life that we no longer regard the cross as a misfortune and incomprehensible meaninglessness but as a sign of your election, as the secret, sure sign that we are yours for ever. For it is a faithful saying that if we die with him we shall also live with him and if we endure with him, we shall also reign with him. Father, we will to share everything with your Son, his life, his divine glory and therefore his suffering and his death. Only with the cross, give the strength to bear it. Cause us to experience in the cross its blessing also. Give us the cross which your wisdom knows is for our salvation and not our ruin.

Son of the Father, Christ who lives in us, you are our hope

of glory. Live in us, bring our life under the laws of your life, make our life like to yours. Live in me, pray in me, suffer in me, more I do not ask. For if I have you I am rich ; those who find you have found the power and the victory of their life. Amen.

NOTE

concerning the contributions in this book

Most of the contributions in this book originally appeared in different publications, as listed below.

THE YEAR OF THE LORD

Advent

The Judgment of the Son of Man: *Der Volksbote* 49 (1949), no. 47, 24 Dec.
The Festival Time of Grace: *ibid.*, no. 48, 1 Dec.
Patience with the Provisional: *ibid.*, no 49, 8 Dec.
The Stumbling-Block of the History of Redemption: *ibid.*, no. 50, 15 Dec.

Christmas

The Answer of Silence: *Die Presse* of 22 Dec. 1962.
The Great Joy: *Der Volksbote* 49 (1949), no. 51, 22 Dec.
Holy Night: previously unpublished.
Grace in the Abysses of Man: first version published in *Die Zeit* 17 (1962), no. 51, 22 Dec.
God's Coming into a Closed World: previously unpublished.

New Year's Eve and New Year's Day

Spiritual Balance-Sheet of a Year: *Geist und Leben* 30 (1957), pp. 406–408.
In the Name of Jesus: *Der Volksbote* 49 (1949), no. 52, 29 Dec.
New Year Meditation: *Stimmen der Zeit* 82 (1956/57), pp. 241–50.

Easter

Beginning of Glory: *Der Volksbote* 56 (1965), no. 14, 1 April.
A Faith that Loves the Earth: *Geist und Leben* 23 (1950), pp. 81–85 (under the title: "Freue dich, Erde, deines himmlischen Lichtes").

Corpus Christi

Feast of the Daily Bread: *Gottes Wort im Kirchenjahr* (1955), pp. 19–21 (under the title: "Mahl der Pilger").
On the Way with the Lord: previously unpublished.
Prayer: printed for the first time in *Offen sei Dein Herz zur Welt,* edited Auguste Staud-Weth (1954), pp. 72–74 (under the title of Whitsun Prayer).

LOVE OF GOD AND THE NEIGHBOUR

The First Commandment: *Der Volksbote* 50 (1950), no. 38, 24 Sept.
The New, Single Precept of Love: lecture at the general meeting of the Catholic Welfare Organization for Girls, Women and Children, 11–13 May 1965 in Cologne, published in *Korrespondenzblatt* 35 (1965), pp. 206–16.
"Forbearing One Another and Forgiving Each Other": sermon at the Northern Catholic Congress in Hamburg, 18 June 1965 ("Service of the Word"). Published in *Geist und Leben* 38 (1965), pp. 310–12.

ONE SPIRIT, MANY GIFTS

Pagan Christians and Christian Pagans: *Der Volksbote* 50 (1950), no. 3, 19 Jan.
The Prophetic Person and the Church: *Münchener Katholische Kirchenzeitung* 41 (1948), no. 7, 15 Feb.
Do Not Evade Decisions! *Kraft und Ohnmacht. Kirche und Glauben in der Erfahrung unserer Zeit,* edited by M. von Galli and M. Plate (For K. Färber on his 75th birthday) (1963), pp. 84–91.
The Christian in the World according to the Fathers: introduction to: *Kirchenväter an Laien. Briefe der Seelenführung,* translated by L. von Welsersheimb (1939; 2nd ed., 1954), pp. 1–17 or 5–12, according to the edition.
The Divine Mystery of Marriage: *Geist und Leben* 31 (1958), pp. 107–9.

SAINTS' DAYS

The Feast-Day of a Holy Beginning: *Korrespondenzblatt des Collegium Canisianum* 94 (1960), pp. 13–16 (originally a meditation outline for 8 Dec. 1959).
Take the Child and his Mother!: *Geist und Leben* 30 (1957), pp. 14–22 (the present version has been much revised).
Thomas Aquinas: *Korrespondenzblatt des Collegium Canisianum* 95 (1961), pp. 25–28.

MYSTERIES OF THE APPARENTLY INSIGNIFICANT

An Ordinary Song: *Orientierung* 23 (1959), pp. 93–94. Postscript to
A. Duval, *Chansons* (Salzburg 1959), pp. 45–46.
Seeing and Hearing: contribution to K. Pawek (editor), *Panoptikum
oder Wirklichkeit. Der Streit um die Photographie* (1965), pp. 75–81.

PRAYER FOR HOPE: previously unpublished.

The author and the publishers are grateful for permission to reproduce
the contributions "Do Not Evade Decisions" and "Hearing and Seeing"
given by the editors and publishers listed.